MW00749582

Stroke

Help From Chinese Medicine

人民卫生出版社
PMPH **PEOPLE'S MEDICAL PUBLISHING HOUSE**

Stroke
Help From Chinese Medicine

Stroke

Help From Chinese Medicine

◉ **Chi Hui-yan, Ph.D TCM**
Carl Stimson, L.Ac

Edited by Ele Denman, L.Ac.
Photographed & Designed by Beijing Sense Media Inc., Ltd

人民卫生出版社
PMPH PEOPLE'S MEDICAL PUBLISHING HOUSE

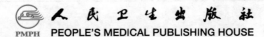

PMPH PEOPLE'S MEDICAL PUBLISHING HOUSE

Website: http://www.pmph.com

Book Title: Stroke- Help From Chinese Medicine
中医科普系列－中风

Copyright © 2011 by People's Medical Publishing House. All rights reserved. No part of this publication may be reproduced, stored in a database or retrieval system, or transmitted in any form or by any electronic, mechanical, photocopy, or other recording means, without the prior written permission of the publisher.

Contact address: No. 19, Pan Jia Yuan Nan Li, Chaoyang District, Beijing 100021, P.R. China, phone/fax: 8610 5978 7338, email: pmph@pmph.com

For text and trade sales, as well as review copy enquiries, please contact PMPH at pmphsales@gmail.com

Disclaimer

This book is for educational and reference purposes only. In view of the possibility of human error or changes in medical science, the author, editor, publisher and any other party involved in the publication of this work do not guarantee that the information contained herein is in any respect accurate or complete. The medicinal therapies and treatment techniques presented in this book are provided for the purpose of reference only. If readers wish to attempt any of the techniques or utilize any of the medicinal therapies contained in this book, the publisher assumes no responsibility for any such actions. It is the responsibility of the readers to understand and adhere to local laws and regulations concerning the practice of these techniques and methods. The authors, editors and publisher disclaim all responsibility for any liability, loss, injury, or damage incurred as a consequence, directly or indirectly, of the use and application of any of the content of this book.

Images in this book are from the Beijing Sense Media Company. It can be contacted at: Phone: 8610 6403 7576, Email: sshg@sshg6688.com

First published: 2011
ISBN: 978-7-117-11621-3/R·11622

Cataloging in Publication Data:
A catalog record for this book is available from the CIP-Database China.

ISBN 978-7-117-11621-3

Printed in The People's Republic of China

Foreword

With development in economy, society and living standards, we do make some progress in treating acute diseases, but we cannot prevent the rising morbidity of some diseases caused by environmental pollution, unhealthy living habits and old age. Moreover, side effects and hazards caused by synthetic drugs are unavoidable.

Cerebrovascular disease (a group of brain dysfunctions related to disease of the blood vessels supplying the brain), well known by its high mortality, high morbidity and high recurrence rate, has become one of the three main causes of human death. It is a severe threat to people's health and life. The sequel of stroke, not only brings great suffering to patients and their families, but also places heavy financial burdens on our society. Traditional Chinese Medicine (TCM) and its rehabilitation therapies are based upon natural medicines and physical treatments; these are becoming more popular as people are learning about these methods and welcoming them.

"Food and medicine have the same origin" is one of the most important concepts of TCM. TCM emphasizes the relationship between food and health, diet and medicine. The fact that the medical science, pharmacology and nutrition are combined in TCM practice reflects this dialectic view. The modern function of food evolves into the medical diet. Recently diet therapy, and understanding the use of food as medicine, has not only attracted attention in China, but has also become fashionable in Japan, Korea, Singapore, and other countries around the world. During the first Asian Medical Diet seminar in 1994, the chairman of the Japanese Medical and Dietetic Treatment Organization said, "People on Okinawa Island are deeply influenced by the Chinese concept that food and medicine have the same origin. They understand this process. People with cardiovascular disease are few, and most people enjoy longevity".

For stroke prevention, treatment and rehabilitation, TCM has many other therapies to offer besides diet therapy. These include acupuncture, cupping, massage, *guā shā*, foot soaks, fumigations and exercise, for example, which are all very special and unique ways to help the recovery from stroke. These methods belong to the category of external treatments, and cause no serious side affects.

In this book we introduce the simplicity and power of the Chinese medical system, and describe a few common therapies to help manage stroke that have proven effective. Although these methods may sound simple and easy to follow, they have at their foundation a profound theory, and require a high level of skill. Anyone interested in these therapies should consult with a professional practitioner in order to gain safe and effective treatment.

Book Guidelines

Explanation

You may be considering Chinese medicine to help manage your stroke, or risk factors associated with stroke, but are unsure of what you will experience during the treatment. Or maybe you have already begun treatment, and wish to know more about the theories and methods used, in order to actively participate in the changes happening to you. If you find yourself in one of these situations, then this is the right book for you. It will give you a better understanding of Chinese medicine, how it can help, and what is involved in treatment. The basic theories will be introduced, and detailed explanations given of methods used by practitioners all around the world. Explanations of commonly known techniques, such as acupuncture and herbal medicine, as well as lesser known modalities like moxibustion and tui na (massage), will help clarify any questions or misconceptions, as well as prepare you for treatment. And lastly, where available, excerpts from modern research and clinical trials are included to inspire confidence in these ancient theories and methods.

Guide

The second purpose of this book is to provide you with a resource that can be used to help implement lifestyle changes that will alleviate symptoms, as well as to increase general health and prevent future illness. There is helpful information on eating habits, exercise programs, and a variety of at-home treatments that are both easy and affordable. From experience, doctors of Chinese medicine know that with proper treatment, the amount and intensity of biomedical intervention necessary can be reduced or even eliminated. It is our hope that with the help of this book as a guide, many medical interventions can be reduced, so that your time, energy, and money can be better spent doing the things you love.

While there is a lot of valuable information in the following chapters, this book is in no way intended to substitute for the care of a trained professional. Making a proper diagnosis and prescribing effective treatments are skills that take years to master, and is especially difficult in complex problems such as stroke. Chinese medicine is a highly individualized system, and the help of a proper guide, especially in the beginning stages of treatment, is essential. For suggestions on how to go about finding a qualified practitioner, please see Appendix.

Table of Contents

Stroke
Help From Chinese Medicine

Chapter 1

Why Chinese Medicine?

Traditional Chinese medicine (TCM), an ancient yet continually developing science, has been used by the Chinese for thousands of years. Now it is more accessible to the world, and is becoming part of the healthcare system. It is widely accepted by the general public and medical workers all over the world. The number of people studying TCM is increasing, as well as the number of people receiving TCM treatments.

Before the opening of Beijing Olympic Games 2008, Yao Ming, a famous Chinese basketball player, received medical surgery for his injured ankle in the USA. Although Yao was recovering as expected after the surgery, the swelling in his left foot was not decreasing. Yao decided to receive TCM treatment to aid his recovery, despite the doctors' doubts. Once he had made his decision, an argument began on the internet between the Chinese and Americans, as to whether Yao should receive TCM treatment or not. Even forums of The Washington Post and Houston Chronicles were involved. Some Americans believed that Yao was taking a gamble with his health before the Olympics. Although Yao could not provide them with an in-depth TCM theory like a specialist could do, in a press conference he firmly stated: "TCM has a long history; it must be effective if the Chinese have been using it for thousands of years. I believe TCM can help me with my injury". Yao was lucky; after some TCM treatment, a very healthy Yao participated in the Beijing Olympics. His

ankle, which had been swollen for a long time before the treatment, healed, and proved the effectiveness of TCM.

There is no doubt that western medicine is amazing. It is incredible for those ancient TCM founding fathers, like Bian Que, Hua Tuo, Zhang Zhong-jing, even to think about X-rays, B-Ultrasonics, enteroscopes, gastroscopes, CTs, MRIs, which are artifacts of cutting-edge technology. However, the miracle of western medicine is just the miracle of technology. The miracle of TCM, on the other hand, is the miracle of the human. The philosophy of TCM is based on human beings, and aims for cures.

With the development of modern medicine, this science has been broken into very tiny parts. A pattern is formed so that patients are treated by a specific specialist, according to the body part which is considered to be dysfunctional. However, this pattern of therapy only focuses on the local pathological change, and neglects the association of all parts of the human body. On the other hand, the theory of TCM emphasizes treating people as a whole.

The human body is not a machine, but a system that has strong self-adjusting ability with which life is supported. The word "health" refers to a balanced status of the system. "Illness", as the opposite, is a disruption to the balance. TCM treatments do not target the disease directly, but focus on the whole system, adjusting it from imbalance into stability. What is usually called "recovery" is actually a combination of homeostasis and the appropriate intervention by doctors.

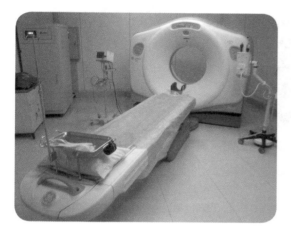

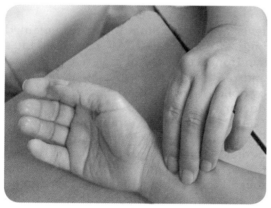

In fact, there are many Olympic athletes who have received TCM treatments and fully recovered. For example, China's National Women's Volleyball team used fumigation treatments to reduce swelling and relieve pain; the Chinese Gymnastics team frequently used massage, acupuncture and moxibustion; Gao Min had her "special foot" reshaped with TCM's bonesetting skills to make her diving more smooth; many football teams frequently visited TCM doctors, and many players recovered after just a few massage treatments. How can TCM be appealing to so many people and cure so many, if it is not effective? Players cannot be fooled because they need a full recovery to continue to compete against the other athletes.

Stroke is a common and hard disease to cure; it is considered one of the top three causes of death in many countries in the world. This disease is a big concern for the medical field because of its high disability, mortality and relapse rates. The ancient Chinese used TCM to treat stroke and accumulated multiple experiences with which they gained a special advantage in the modern medicine world. It is not that western medicine is negligent in treating stroke, because in the early stage of this disease good western medical care is needed. If patients can receive a combination therapy of both TCM and western medicine wisely, then the disability, mortality and relapse rate can be reduced, and the patient's life quality can be increased.

Let's get familiar with TCM's concepts by the following real life cases.

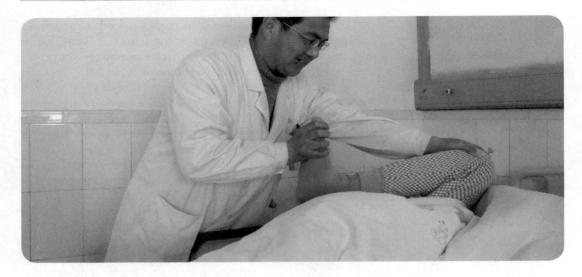

Case 1

In May.10, 2002, Liu Hai-ruo, a presenter on Phoenix TV, was seriously injured traveling from London to Cambridge, when the train derailed. Her two travel mates died instantly, and she was declared "brain dead" by the hospital. On the same day she was transported to Beijing by the International SOS to receive treatment. A group of specialists were waiting there to perform a series of tests on her; the results did not look good. Liu had chest and neck fractures, and blood in her urine from damage to the kidneys. The MRI examination indicated there were hemorrhagic infarcts in the midbrain and both sides of her brain. She was given a high dose of antibiotics, but both her fever and intracranial pressure remained high. According to TCM specialists, Liu's syndrome consisted of a high fever, coma, and red tongue with no coat, all of which complied with the term "*rè*" in TCM. The doctor on duty decided to prescribe *Ān Gōng Niú Huáng Wán* immediately, which is one of the three most effective Chinese herbal formulas in treating coma. It was dissolved and taken via a nasal feeding tube. It took 7 doses to relieve the high fever and coma. Directly after that the medical team employed rehabilitation therapies like acupuncture, massage, and Chinese herbs to help her regain consciousness. She finally opened her eyes after a month of intensive treatment.

Liu's family was very happy for her revival. Once they did not follow the doctor's advice and fed her too much. This caused an intestinal obstruction because the food could not be digested. The advice from western medicine was to use a gastro-intestinal decompression tube to expel the gastric juices and gas; but that would cause electrolytes to be lost, which would compromise Liu's recovery. Eventually TCM specialists helped save her life by prescribing the Chinese herbal formula *Lǐ Zhōng Yì Qì Tāng* to take internally, and massaging her abdomen, and then finally prescribing her sesame oil to take internally.

5 months later, Liu was moved from ICU and began to receive rehabilitation therapy. During the rehabilitation course, Chinese doctors used acupuncture, massage, and Chinese herbs to help restore her body and language functions. She returned to work sooner than was expected.

It is unbelievable that 100 days after the accident, Liu Hai-ruo, who had been declared "brain dead" by British medical professions, finally regained consciousness and even her speech. Now she is not only able to write and talk, but also to walk and work!

Liu Hai-ruo's father said that he did not believe in TCM previously, but the facts changed his mind; both his daughters were saved by TCM. The eldest daughter suffered infertility due to brain tumors, but was cured through TCM treatment and had

a baby. Liu Hai-ruo was brought back to life by the combination of TCM and western medicine. Liu Hai-ruo's eldest sister said: "We were lucky to be able to return to a Chinese hospital where Chinese medicine and herbs are used. Liu was saved by the thorough combination between Chinese and western medicine, as was I".

"I always want to go back to that British hospital and let them know my current situation; they will surely be very surprised," said Liu Hai-ruo in an interview.

Although "brain dead" is not recognized in TCM terms, TCM has treated coma patients as a result of stroke for many years, and have accumulated much experience. Chinese medicine played an important part in saving Liu Hai-ruo's life.

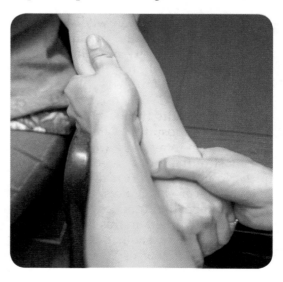

Case 2

Ms. Lin, 42 years old, is a top leader of a transnational corporation. Once she had spoken too much in preparation for an important conference, and lost her voice just before the conference day. She was a major speaker at the conference, so she took antibiotics, but without any results. She thought that the conference might be ruined, so she tried to send a message to a TCM doctor (because she was unable to speak) asking for help. The doctor went to see her at 10 o'clock that night and treated her with acupuncture. Ms. Lin regained her voice the next day.

Case 3

In 2003, SARS spread wildly throughout China. It originated in Guangzhou. Guangzhou University of Chinese Medicine First Affiliated Hospital identified a treatment method for SARS using western medicine and TCM therapy to treat patients. The results turned out to be very effective. The hospital treated 36 patients with SARS in total; there were no deaths, and most of them recovered without any further complications. The average time of relieving fever was 3 days, and the average hospitalization time less than 9 days. No medical workers in this hospital were infected. However, another case worth our consideration is that of Ye Xin and Deng Qiu-yun, two head nurses of Guangzhou University of Chinese Medicine Second Affiliated Hospital, both infected by SARS, who received different treatments. Ye Xin took antibiotics from the moment she was infected by SARS, but there was no sign of recovery and eventually she passed away. Deng Qiu-yun used antibiotics initially, but then stopped to begin TCM therapy with a well known, old, TCM specialist and eventually she made a full recovery. When SARS finally went, many patients who had survived began to suffer from osteonecrosis of the femoral head, or osteoporosis, due to long term abuse of hormones, and eventually they could no longer use their legs.

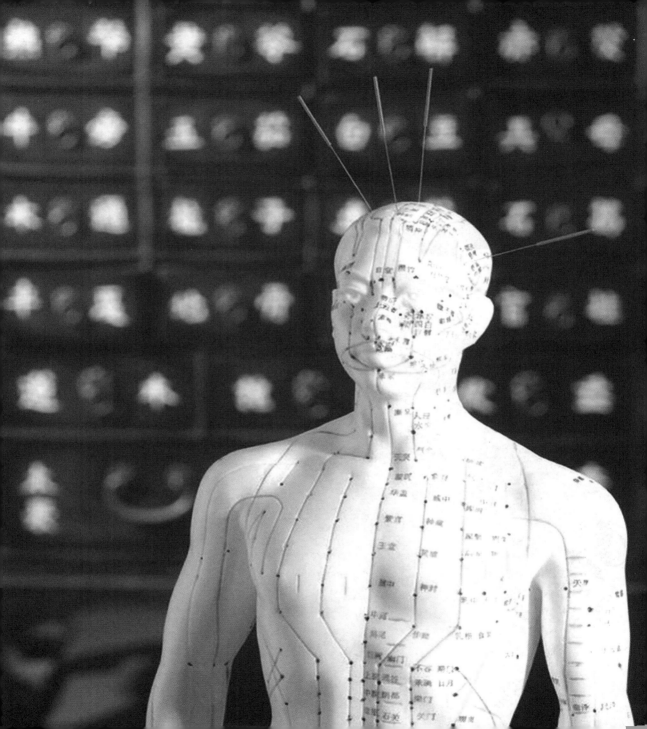

Stroke

Help From Chinese Medicine

Chapter 2

How Does Chinese Medicine Understand Stroke Management?

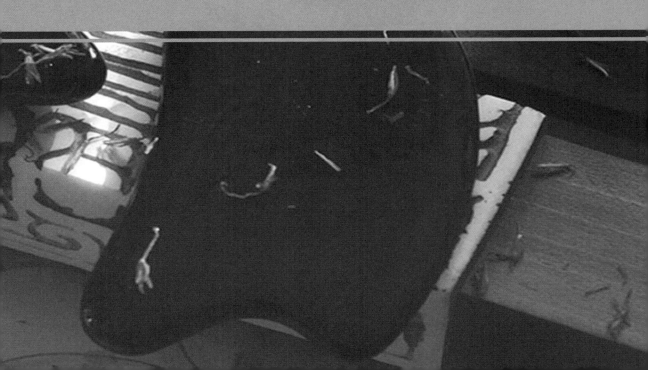

Many people in western countries are under the impression that Chinese medicine and acupuncture involve some kind of sorcery with needles or mysterious spirits. And indeed the ancient language of Chinese medicine can reinforce this view by referring to the "spirits" of the heart, lungs, liver, etc., or by insisting on the existence of the *jīng luò*, which is the network that runs throughout the human body and is responsible for transporting qi and blood. However, to wise doctors and open-minded patients, the words used matter little, what is important is if the underlying concepts are able to be applied and beneficial results obtained.

Heracleum Hemsleyanum Diels

Chinese Medicine Introduction

What is the difference between Traditional Chinese medicine (TCM) and western medicine (WM), and their relationship to the earth? These may be important questions for many people who do not understand Chinese medicine, and it seems that only when we answer these questions, can we truly know what Traditional Chinese medicine is.

There is an apparent distinction between TCM and WM. A full awareness of their distinction is beneficial not only in understanding the basic concepts involved in TCM, but also in recognizing and applying it.

1. Origin of the Difference between Traditional Chinese Medicine and Westerr Medicine

Ever since man has existed on earth, he has experienced injury and disease. Animals have certain instinctive measures that provide immediate cures. For example, wounded animals often lick their wounds to alleviate pain and bleeding, and a poisoned cat usually eats a great deal of grass to initiate vomiting. This is also the case in the instinctive behavior of primitive people. Moreover, the nearer to the primitive state human beings were, the more practical these instincts were. At this stage, there was no difference between TCM and WM, which both could be called "instinctive medical behavior".

Good at memorizing and accumulating experience, man differs from animals in their ability to use the experience of others for reference, and to discover cures through accidental events. For instance, toothache could be eased by accidentally touching LI 4 (*hé gǔ*, 合谷) area; constipation could be alleviated by accidentally tasting *dà huáng* (Radix et Rhizoma Rhei). Over tens of thousands of years' accumulated experience, people were able to ascertain therapeutic methods corresponding to various symptoms, which had been passed on through oral instruction. Then, there was still no gap between traditional Chinese medicine and western medicine, which both could be called "empirical medicine".

When human beings evolved to the stage where he was capable of thinking, he became curious about the causes of injury, disease, and recovery. At that time people were convinced that superhuman powers such as gods, ghosts and demons existed in the unseen world, who governed nature, health and disease. The threat of natural phenomena and the prevalence of infectious diseases were believed to be human's punishment from the gods, ghosts and demons. Consequently, in order to avoid disaster people attempted to seek help from

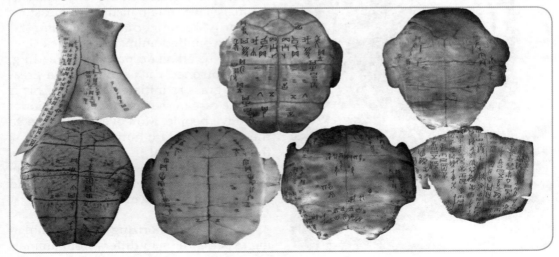

the gods and ghosts; in order to prevent and treat diseases they created many rituals to appease the gods and ghosts, or to defeat demons. Their methods were mainly through songs, dances, sacrifices, prayers, blessings, incantations and so on. Up until this period there was still no distinction between Chinese and western medicine, both of which could be called "witch medicine" or "magic medicine" on the basis of inaccurate knowledge.

With the invention of the written word, Chinese characters, people set out to rearrange the previous empirical and witch medicine, recording them by script, and gradually combining them. The ancient medical behavior and medicine evolved into the era of "recorded medicine". At this time people already had a vast knowledge; they recorded many facts on human morphology, life phenomena, and accumulated rich experience in prevention and treatment of disease. However, they were still short of theoretical explanation. To further understand human life and disease, the eastern and western medical circles assimilated philosophies from their advanced cultures of the time, and each established their own theoretical system.

Chinese philosophers believed that the origin of material in the world was "original qi". Original qi is unstructured chaos, and has features such as supermorphology, continuity, motility, vagueness and subsequently inseparability. Additionally, there exists movements of intrinsic contradiction within original qi, and accordingly the force of movement and change lay inside the object itself. Yet western philosophers held that the material origin of the world was atoms. Atoms are the scattered material particles and the origin constituting objects and the world. They include features like substance, morphology and independence. There are no movements of intrinsic contradiction within an atom. It is the external force that produces the formation and movement of an object.

Such diversity in eastern and western philosophies exerted a tremendous impact on medicine. Not only did it provide different academic and thinking foundations for Chinese and western medicine, but also resulted in the unique theoretical systems of Chinese and western medicine. From then on, the two medicines diverged from each other and advanced in their own ways.

2. Differences between TCM and WM

Western medicine attaches importance to structure, morphology, substance and antagonism, as well as to the understanding of life emphatically, by means of reduction and analysis from the perspective of microcosm and morphology. Therefore local structural and pathological changes are specifically emphasized in the understanding of disease. According to western medicine, pathological changes are based on parenchymatous changes of local organs and the idealistic indexes. Signs and symptoms of local organs are the major basis for diagnosis, resulting in many levels of examinations, and analysis of the specific diseased organs. Western medicine's roots are founded in anatomy and are compatible with modern scientific technology, so it is readily understood and accepted.

Traditional Chinese medicine pays attention to functional state, correlation and unity, as well as to the understanding of life emphatically by means of systematic analysis from the perspective of macrocosm and dynamics. Consequently, overall functional and pathological changes are especially emphasized in the understanding of disease. It attaches the same importance to the local imbalance of organs, as to the overall imbalance of the whole body. It takes clinical symptoms and signs as its major basis for diagnosis, and focuses especially on the synthetic judgment of the state of the local and the whole. Since its cognitive methods are based on ancient Chinese philosophy, it is challenging for TCM to try and assimilate with modern scientific technology; it is not always easy for TCM to be understood and accepted.

In fact, a great deal of anatomical research had already been conducted in the field of TCM in the Pre-qin Period, which was recorded clearly in both *The Inner Classic* (*Nèi Jīng*) and *The Classic of Difficult Issues* (*Nàn Jīng*). For example, the research of the length, morphology, and capacity of the digestive organs as well as the size, location and texture of viscera. Although limited by the conditions of the time, this anatomical knowledge appeared quite shallow, but actually already far exceeded research at this time, and laid the morphological foundation for the formation of the theory of visceral manifestation. However, it was difficult practically, because it did not focus on anatomical structure but on the functional state, and because such gross anatomy could not directly serve clinical diagnosis and treatment of the time; neither could it explain mechanisms of the actions of drugs in treating diseases, or guide the clinical prescriptions. Therefore, TCM did not depend on it entirely, continue research on it, or develop it much; but on the basis of clinical practice, from the concept of the unity of man and nature, TCM took the theories of original qi, yin-yang and five elements as its theoretical tools, established a series of systems of treatment based on syndrome differentiation like *zang-fu* organ syndrome differentiation, six-meridian syndrome differentiation, qi-blood syndrome differentiation, and body fluid syndrome differentiation, and gradually made its way toward the study of functional pathology.

3. The Concept of Visceral Manifestation Differences in TCM and WM

There is a concept of five *zang* which include liver, heart, spleen, lung, kidney in Chinese medicine. However, what is the difference between the term five "*zang*" in TCM and "organ" in WM?

As for "internal organs" in western anatomy, it is borrowed from the corresponding names of viscera in TCM, referring to the entities and structures of internal organs, similar to the concept of viscera in traditional Chinese medicine, but completely different from the systematic concept of visceral manifestation.

"Viscera" is an anatomical concept, specifically referring to the anatomical entities of the internal organs, including the morphology and location of five *zang* organs, six *fu* organs and extraordinary *fu* organs. Whereas "visceral manifestation", based on the anatomical concept of viscera and the observations of physiological and pathological changes, in the light of theories of yin-yang and five elements, is an systematic understanding of five constituents, five sense organs and five emotions of the human body, as well as the five orientations, five annual divisions and five climatic factors in the natural world. It is a comprehensive concept of visceral morphology, location, physiological functions and pathological changes, the inter-relations of viscera and the unity between viscera and their external environments. Thus, the concept of visceral manifestation includes the concept of viscera and fully represents the unique thinking way of TCM.

The concept of "internal organs", based upon the dissection and description of entities, is a morphological structure, and their functions can be perceived by direct anatomical analysis. Whereas the concept of visceral manifestation stresses a macro-generalization of visceral functions, and is a comprehensive structure including both the morphological basis, and the functions constructed out of it. Although its formation depends on morphology, the observation of the overall functions of the human body plays a major role in the evolution of this theory. Physiological functions and pathological phenomena of a certain system, are summarized within visceral manifestation in TCM, so the concept of visceral manifestation in TCM cannot be equated to the organs of the same name in the modern anatomical physiology.

Viscera refer to five physiological and pathological systems based on five *zang* organs.

Case

If a man catches pneumonia and goes to see WM doctor, the doctor will put him through a series of examinations to discover whether the infectious agents are bacterial or viral, and whether to use antibiotics or antivirals to kill them, thus curing the disease. That is the main treatment that WM has developed.

In contrast, TCM believes that virus and bacteria exist in the natural world. Infectious agents will not survive and thrive when people are in good health. TCM theory says "If a person is in good state, thus yin and yang are balanced, (s)he cannot be ill even if extraordinary weather changes are encountered; if the balance is broken, (s)he will be ill because the body cannot protect itself". When TCM treats these diseases, they usually use herbal prescriptions recorded two thousand years ago in *Treatise on Cold Damage* (*Shāng Hán Lùn*). *Má Xìng Shí Gān Tāng* (麻杏石甘汤, Ephedra, Apricot Kernel, Gypsum and Licorice Decoction), for example, is one of these prescriptions. Why is it still effective in treating pneumonia? Western Medicine does not believe that the *Má Xìng Shí Gān Tāng* can kill the bacteria or virus at all, but here lays the magic of TCM. The dose is ineffective when in the bottle, or as loose herbs, but once drunk it begins to work. Why? Because it uses the variation of itself to rectify the variation of human body, thus improving the body's internal environment and removing those infectious agents. If we can understand TCM this way, then we discover the scientific nature hidden in it.

Key Concepts in TCM

The theoretical system of TCM is characterized by the concepts of holism and yin-yang theory.

1. The Concept of Holism

The concept of holism is the interpretation of TCM with the integrity of the human body itself, and the unity of man, nature and social environments. Holism is the guidance under which the ancient Chinese understood nature and phenomena, whereas the concept of holism in TCM is the guidance under which physicians of TCM interpret life phenomena and treat diseases. It is not a stop gap measure, but places more emphasis on treating the human body as a complete organism. It advocates that human beings are part of nature and society, and that health is an integration of both physical and mental well-being, which correlates to WHO's definition of health re-released in 1990. Natural therapies in the healthcare model advocate a correspondence with nature, a connection between nature and human beings, and recommend returning to basics and to nature; the emphasis on humans and nature, social harmony and unity. This is echoed by modern medicine's "biological - psychological - social" model.

(1) Integrity of the human body

◆ Organic wholeness of the human body

The human body is composed of various tissues and organs, including five *zang* organs, six *fu* organs, qi, blood, fluids, channels, body constituents, sense organs and orifices, four limbs and all the skeletal parts. Though distinct in structure and function, the *zang-fu* organs work together i.e., they interrelate, coordinate and inter-act with each other, to maintain the life activities of the human body. Physiologi-cally, the five physiological systems of the human body, namely the cardiac, hepatic, splenic, pulmonary and renal systems, center on the five *zang* organs, and con-nect with the six *fu* organs, the five con-stituents, as well as the sense organs and orifices through the network of channels.

◆ **Unity of the physical body and spirit**

The physical body and spirit are the two essential elements of life activities. Their unity ensures the existence of life. In the long course of life they are insepara-ble; supporting and complementing each other. Spirit accommodates itself within

the physical body. Without the physi-cal, spirit cannot exist. Where there is physicality, there is spirit. Spirit is the life manifestation of the physical, governing the physical and all life activities. It means that one's health composes both physical health and mental health.

(2) Integral association of humans and nature

Humans live in the natural world. Unavoidably, man is influenced by natu-ral changes and makes the corresponding changes to adapt to his changing external environmental. For example, the chang-ing of the four seasons affect physiological functions of the human body. Generally speaking, in summer, since qi and blood flow quicker due to the hot weather, there are rapid, surging pulses, profuse sweat-ing and scanty urination. On the contrary, in winter, since qi and blood moves slow-er due to the cold weather, there are deep, slow pulses, frequent urination and scanty sweating.

Additionally, the changes of nature impose great influences upon the patho-logical state of the human body. For in-stance, humans are prone to be attacked by seasonal and epidemic diseases. The symptoms of arthralgia are usually aggra-vated in autumn and winter, or on cloudy and rainy days.

Geographical difference also af-fects the physiological and pathological states of the body. Man lives amongst the clean air, sunshine, rain, dew, animals and plants in nature. Different localities bear different climates and products. Accordingly, people in various areas are characterized by different constitutions and onset of disease. The so called "non-acclimatization" is due to temporary unadaptability to the climate, and other environmental factors of a new place.

(3) Integral association of humans and his social environment

Man lives in a complicated social environment, where his social status, economical conditions and personal relations are constantly changing. Therefore physiological activities and pathological changes of the body are inevitably affected by his social environment. Generally speaking, favorable social conditions and harmonious personal relationships are beneficial to a sound mind, a healthy body and recovery of disease. Contrarily, unhappy social conditions and tense personal relationships make people depressed and apprehensive, thus harming the mind and body, and aggravating disease.

Clinical link: family quarrels, death of family members, unemployment and bankruptcy often aggravate the conditions of patients who suffer from coronary heart disease, hypertension and tumors.

Therefore, according to the theory of medicine and health preservation, we must follow the concept of holism, which is simple and closely linked with the theory of modern medicine, in order to better understand diseases and their treatments.

Case

We use the Liu Hai-ruo's example as mentioned above to introduce the concept of yin-yang balance and holism in TCM. That is, to treat her overall person and focus on the balance of her body system, to gain effective results.

Liu Hai-ruo had a high fever twice during the course of treatment. In that situation, her persistent high fever could easily have depleted her organs, and she may have failed to recover. In order to control the infection as quickly as possible, the doctor gave her a high dosage of antibiotics over a very short time. However, this led to other problems: flora imbalance, fungal infections, and bacteria in the blood. Then the high fever returned. Her blood pressure dropped, until she was almost in shock. The situation was so extreme that the use of antibiotics had to be modified. There were two options: the WM doctors wanted to use nystatin, which has side effects on the liver. The dilemma was that Liu's liver had already been damaged, causing serious liver dysfunction; it would be unpredictable to use nystatin in this situation. The other option, suggested by TCM doctors, was to use Chinese herbs like allicin and *Yú Xīng Căo* (Herba Houttuyniae, heartleaf houttuynia herb), which were effective, cheaper, as well as having no side effects on the liver. Eventually they agreed to use allicin and switch to another type of antibiotics, with nystatin as a backup if required. In fact, after four days the fever had gone.

Therefore, why should we reject a treatment if it is beneficial to patients. Why shouldn't we integrate the medicines if they result in a safer and more effective treatment for the patient? As in Hai-ruo's example, TCM was not used exclusively, but as a very important part of the therapy that reduced many side effects of WM. Hai-ruo has been using Chinese herbs regularly. Her face, which was previously distorted by the damage to her brainstem, has almost fully recovered due to long term acupuncture treatments.

2. Yin–Yang

(1) Concept of yin and yang

Yin and yang belong to the category of ancient Chinese philosophy. It is a general term for two opposite aspects of something, or some phenomena in nature, which interrelate with each other. The original meaning of yin and yang was quite simple, merely referring to the sunny and shady sides of a mountain: the side exposed to the sun pertained to yang, whereas the side opposite the sun, the shady side, pertained to yin. In that sense, yin and yang had nothing to do with philosophy.

With the development of human life and productive practice, the observational range was gradually broadened, and the naive connotation of yin and yang was subsequently extended. For example, since it was bright and warm in the sunny place while dim and cold in the shady place, brightness and warmth were categorized into yang, and dimness and cold into yin. This categorization was further extended in the following way: in terms of day and night, day was bright and warm while night was dim and cold, so day pertained to yang and night to yin;

animals including human beings were excited and active in warm, bright places, and inhibited and still in dim, cold places, so activeness and excitement pertained to yang, while stillness and inhibition to yin. As a result of such an infinite extension, almost all things and phenomena in nature could be categorized into yin or yang aspects, which could be used to analyze and deduce those that could not be easily perceived. Then yin and yang no longer specifically referred to the sunny and shady sides. They had evolved into an abstract concept, used to generalize things, or phenomena, opposite to each other in nature.

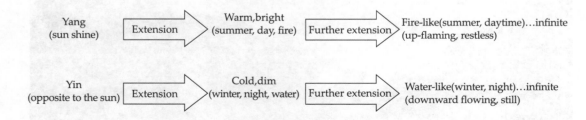

Yang (sun shine) → Extension → Warm,bright (summer, day, fire) → Further extension → Fire-like(summer, daytime)…infinite (up-flaming, restless)

Yin (opposite to the sun) → Extension → Cold,dim (winter, night, water) → Further extension → Water-like(winter, night)…infinite (downward flowing, still)

Examples of Yin-Yang Categorization

Category	Yang	Yin
Time	Day	Night
Space	Heaven	Earth
Season	Spring, Summer	Autumn, Winter
Temperature	Hot	Cold
Weight	Light	Heavy
Speed	Fast	Slow
Motion	Up and out, vigorous	Down and in, subtle
Brightness	Light	Dark
Sex	Male	Female
Tissue and organs	Skin, hair	Bone, tendon
Disease	Acute	Chronic

In order to understand yin-yang's properties, several points have to be taken into consideration.

➤ The theory of yin and yang is merely used to define the nature of two correlated objects or two aspects within a single object. If two objects do not correlate with each other, or if two opposite aspects do not belong to one entity, their relative properties and relationships cannot be discriminated by this theory. For example, day and night both belong to the category of time and oppose to each other, so they can be generalized as yang and yin. But day and earth do not belong to the same category, neither correlating with, nor opposing to each other, so the relationship between day and earth cannot be explained with yin-yang properties.

➤ Yin-yang properties of things are not absolute but relative. Under given conditions, yin-yang properties of things may transform into its opposite. Under given conditions, a cold syndrome of yin property can transform into a heat syndrome of yang property, and vice versa. For example, external contraction of pathogenic cold (catching a cold) will cause yin-cold syndrome, manifested as aversion of cold, and clear nasal discharge. If not treated effectively, cold will transform into heat, which will be accompanied by a high fever, thirst, constipation, and yellow nasal discharge.

➢ Opposition and restriction between yin and yang means that yin and yang, opposite in nature, struggle against, restrain and repel each other. For example, warmth and heat may dispel cold, whereas coolness and cold may lower a high temperature.

(2) The theory of yin and yang used in TCM

As a theoretical tool, the theory of yin and yang permeates through all aspects of the theoretical system of TCM, used extensively to explain morphology, structure, physiological functions and pathological changes of the human body, and guiding clinical diagnosis and treatment, as well as health preservation.

◆ To explain morphology and structure of the human body

The human body is an organic whole composed of viscera, channels, constituents, sense organs and orifices, qi, blood, and fluids. They are all expressions of the unity and oppositional relationships between yin and yang inside the human body, which attribute each part of the body to yin or yang properties. In terms of general location, the upper is yang and the lower is yin; the exterior is yang and the interior is yin; the back is yang and the abdomen is yin; the lateral aspects of the extremities are yang and the medial aspects are yin.

◆ To explain physiological functions of the human body

With respect to normal life activities of the human body, both the whole and its various components can be generalized and explained by the theory of yin and yang. Normal life activities of the human body virtually result from the coordination between yin and yang in a unity of opposites. For example, qi which maintains the life activities of the human body can be classified into yin qi and yang qi, according to its physiological functions.

Yin qi governs coolness, moistening, stillness, inhibition and descending; while yang qi, governs warmth, promotion, excitement and ascending. It is because yin qi and yang qi stay in a state of balance and coordination by means of opposition, restriction, interdependence, complementation and inter-transformation that life activities can be performed in order.

◆ To explain pathological changes of the human body

Equilibrium and coordination of yin and yang in the human body, is the essential condition for the maintenance of normal life activities; yin-yang disharmony is the root cause of the onset and development of disease. Therefore, though intricate, the mechanism and change of disease can be generally analyzed, summarized and explained with the theory of yin and yang.

The formation and development of diseases involve aspects of both healthy and pathogenic qi. Healthy qi and pathogenic qi, as well as their interaction, can all be generalized and explained by the theory of yin and yang. The healthy qi can be divided into two aspects of yin and yang, namely yin qi and yang qi; while the pathogenic qi can be also divided into two aspects of yin and yang, namely yin pathogens and yang pathogens. When yin pathogens cause disease, yang is likely to be damaged; when yang pathogens cause disease, yin is likely to be damaged. So the course of a disease is actually the process of the struggle between the healthy and pathogenic qi that consequently results in yin-yang disharmony in the human body, mainly manifested as the following four aspects: preponderance of yin or yang, or decline of yin or yang.

Manifestations of Yin-yang Disorders

	Typical Manifestations
Yang excess	Fever, aversion to heat, thirst, desire for cold drinks, red complexion, restlessness, yellow-colored mucus, dark-colored urination, constipation, red tongue, yellow tongue coating, rapid pulse
Yin excess	Aversion to cold, no thirst, desire for warm drinks, thin and watery mucus, loose stools, pale complexion, light-colored tongue, white tongue coating, slow or tense pulse
Yang deficiency	Preference for warmth, cold limbs, pale complexion, spontaneous sweating, fatigue, shortness of breath, loose stools, enlarged and light-colored tongue, white tongue coating, deep, slow and weak pulse
Yin deficiency	Thirst, dry mouth and throat, hot feeling in the soles and palms, afternoon fever, night sweating, red tongue with little coating, rapid and fine pulse

◆ To treat disease

It means that the theory of yin and yang can be used to determine the therapeutic principles and to generalize properties and actions of Chinese herbs. Yin-yang disharmony is one of the basic mechanisms of disease, and preponderance and decline of yin or yang are the basic manifestations. Accordingly, it is one of the basic therapeutic principles to reestablish a state of relative coordination and equilibrium by regulating yin and yang, supplementing insufficiency and reducing excess.

(3) Reduce excess

It applies to excess syndrome resulting mostly from preponderance of yin or yang. Specifically, excess-heat syndrome caused by preponderance of yang should be treated by the therapeutic principle of releasing heat to reduce the preponderant yang; excess-cold syndrome caused by preponderance of yin should be treated by the therapeutic principle of dispelling cold to reduce the excessive yin.

(4) Tonify insufficiency

It applies to deficiency syndrome resulting mostly from decline of yin or yang. Specifically, deficiency-cold syndrome caused by decline of yang should be treated by the therapeutic principle of warming yang to replenish the impaired yang; deficiency-heat syndrome caused by decline of yin should be treated by the therapeutic principle of nourishing yin to notify the insufficient yin.

Therapeutic principles of regulating yin and yang

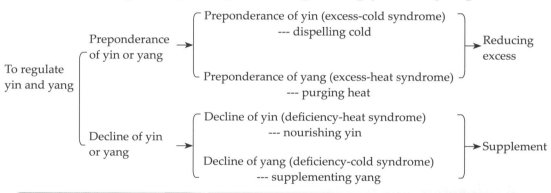

To regulate yin and yang

Preponderance of yin or yang →
- Preponderance of yin (excess-cold syndrome) --- dispelling cold
- Preponderance of yang (excess-heat syndrome) --- purging heat

→ Reducing excess

Decline of yin or yang →
- Decline of yin (deficiency-heat syndrome) --- nourishing yin
- Decline of yang (deficiency-cold syndrome) --- supplementing yang

→ Supplement

(5) Life cultivation guidelines ⟳

The significance of preserving health is to build up one's constitution, promote longevity, and to prevent or avoid disease.

Under the guidance of the concept of holism, it is held in health preservation of TCM that all life activities of the human body should conform to the waning-waxing and inter-transformation laws of yin and yang in the four seasons, in order to regulate the yin and yang of the body. For instance, in spring and summer, in accordance with sprouting and growth in the natural world, yang qi of the body should be preserved to benefit birth and growth of the body; in autumn and winter, in accordance with reaping and storing, yin qi of the body should be preserved to benefit storage of essential qi.

The Yellow Emperor's Inner Classic (*Huáng Dì Nèi Jīng*) stressed again and again that man corresponds with heaven and earth, with the four seasons, and nature. It recognized the ebbs and flows, the rhythms of the earth where man resides; in essence, it is the rhythm of life that is formed by the cyclical changes of solar radiation on earth.

The Spiritual Pivot (*Líng Shū*) stated, "To come in spring, to grow in summer, to be harvested in autumn, and to be stored in winter. It is the nature of the qi, and humans should correspond with it. With spouting, growth, harvesting and storing of the four seasons in a year, a person's physical activities are changed along with the season. When a doctor treats, he makes corresponding changes not only according to individual conditions, but also according to local environment and seasonal variations."

3. Inborn and Acquired Constitution

What is called one's inborn constitution is the original qi of a newborn baby that is acquired from the essence and blood of its parents, and is the essential substance of life. It compliments the acquired constitution. The kidney is the source of reproduction and development, and it is said that, "The kidney rules the inborn constitution," and, "The kidney is the root of the inborn constitution." The acquired constitution refers to the spleen and stomach, because they provide the body with the substance and energy necessary to maintain life by their digestion, absorption and transportation of food. So it is said, "The spleen and stomach are the acquired foundation."

Stroke in TCM

named *"bào jué"* and *"piān kū"* can be deduced as stroke by their symptoms, but the term *"zhòng fēng"* (stroke) did not appear in the book. For example, the term *"pú jī piān kū"* in the book *Basic Questions* (*Sù Wèn*,素问), means falling down unconscious, resulting in hemiplegia.

Stroke, also known as cerebral apoplexy, is the common name of acute cerebrovascular disease in TCM. It is a collection of diseases whose major symptoms include sudden collapse, unconsciousness, distorted mouth, difficulty in speech and hemiplegia. It is divided into two categories: hemorrhagic stroke and ischemic stroke.[1,2]

Records related to stroke can be found in *The Yellow Emperor's Inner Classic* written 2000 years ago. The diseases

It is the book *Essentials from the Golden Cabinet* (*Jīn Guì Yào Lüè*, 金匮要略) in which this disease was formally named stroke. The book, written by Zhang Zhong-jing in the Donghan dynasty, dedicates a chapter to this disease. The author summarized two main characteristics. Firstly, the serious disease is caused by the rapid progression. Secondly, the disease is accompanied by hemiplegia, and a distorted face. These descriptions are basically the same as the symptoms of stroke.

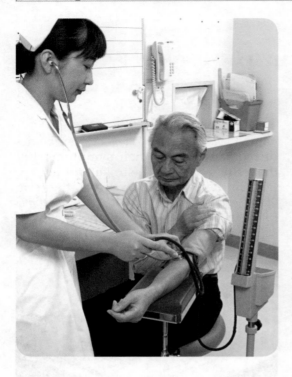

1. The Cause of Stroke

TCM believes that the main causes of stroke are: wind (environmental and climatic), phlegm (overweight, high blood pressure, high blood lipids, and diabetes, caused by an unhealthy diet), *yū* (thrombosis or unsmooth blood flow), weakness (heredity or exhaustion after birth), and internal injury caused by excess of the seven emotions (sudden high blood pressure caused by emotions)[3], which match the opinion of modern medicine.

(1) Wind 𝒞

Wind, one of the six qi from a TCM perspective, originally referred to the climate. The growth of all things depends upon the ordinary climatic changes, which cause no harm because the body has learned to adjust itself to these changes. Thus the normal six "qi" generally do not cause illness in people.

However, if the climatic changes are abnormal, such as the six qi being in excess, or falling below the appropriate level, qi is not what is expected at that time of year (spring turning cold instead of being warm, the winter turning hot instead of being cool), or the weather changing too rapidly (suddenly cold or suddenly hot), then it will be difficult for people to make the necessary adjustments and could lead to illness. Therefore the six abnormal qi, which have been turned from harmlessness into pathogenic factors, are called six excesses or six pathogens. Accordingly, the abnormal wind that leads to illness is called "wind pathogen". When people lack healthy qi their resistance decreases, and so the wind pathogen can invade and lead to stroke. For example, a cold winter may stimulate the sympathetic nervous system, while extremely hot weather may excite the central nervous system, and dry air may dehydrate the body and cause hypovolemia (a decrease in blood volume). These wind pathogens cause stroke by disturbing the vascular regulation system.

are the characteristics of wind, and therefore called "Stroke". In TCM, wind is a complex factor causing disease, and is divided into external and internal wind, according to their pathogenic characteristics.

External wind is caused by abnormal climatic changes, and can cause disease. Internal wind refers to the pathological changes caused by visceral dysfunction in the development of disease, which are similar to those resulting from the attack of wind.

The characteristics of wind, in nature and pathogenically, are mobile and rapid changes. "Mobile" implies that pathogenic wind tends to move constantly, causing diseases that move around. "Rapid changes" denotes that disease caused by wind is characterized by a sudden attack and is constantly changing.

The clinical features of stroke include a rapid onset and quick changes, which

Wind stirring inside refers to the morbid condition resulting from visceral dysfunction, marked by movement, dizziness, convulsion, and tremors. Clinically, there are symptoms with stroke such as frequent headaches, dizziness, convulsions, limb tremors, and paralysis. This is what leads Chinese medicine practitioners to believe that stroke reflects "wind stirring inside".

Since wind is closely related to the liver, it is also known as "stirring of liver wind".

Transformation of liver yang into wind is the result of deficient yin failing to restrain yang due to emotional changes, or to overstrain that consumes liver yin and kidney yin, leading to abnormal rising of liver yang. In addition to the symptoms of hyperactivity of liver yang, there are manifestations of muscular twitching and cramp, numbness in the extremities, dizziness, facial distortion, hemiplegia, or even unconsciousness in severe cases. Stroke may attack patients with hypertension, which is due to the transformation of liver yang into wind, caused by extreme emotional changes.

(2) Phlegm and dampness

Phlegm is a common English word, with a slightly different meaning in Chinese medicine. It includes both tangible phlegm and what is called intangible phlegm. The former is the common mucous that is secreted from the respiratory tract, sometimes in large quantities when someone is sick. The latter is the unhealthy product of a disturbance in water metabolism. It is thick and turbid, and stagnates in the organs, channels and tissues of the body. It can be detected during physical examination as chronic swollen lymph nodes, subcutaneous nodules, and other semi-hard swellings.

When the lung and throat are infected, their secretions are tangible phlegm. While in diseases such as extreme emotional disturbances or strokes, the main cause is due to phlegm blocking the channels of the mind. This is referred to as intangible phlegm. Strange and difficult diseases often involve phlegm according to the theory of Chinese medicine[4].

In modern medicine, some research indicates that people with a high glucose and fat intake, as well as a high calorie intake, are prone to obesity, hypertension, hyperlipidemia, and diabetes mellitus. All the diseases mentioned above, are clinical factors which can induce stroke[5,6].

(3) Stagnant blood

Stagnant blood refers to the pathological output of a block in the blood circulation, including an obstruction in the channels and *zang-fu*. Once an obstruction has formed it becomes a new etiological factor. For the reasons mentioned above, both ischemic stroke and hemorrhagic stroke are in the category of stagnant blood[7].

For example, cerebral infarction of stroke is due to the obstruction of blood circulation in the cerebral blood vessels, and results in the whole blood vessel network being blocked by the obstruction of one mere vessel. The cerebral hemorrhage is induced by the rupture of a blood vessel, and causes blood to spill into the extravascular space. The ruptured blood vessel does not allow blood to flow, and the other vessels are blocked by the compressed brain tissue. From this viewpoint, the obstruction of blood is not only a pathological product, but also a risk factor of disease, with potentially very serious effects. Therefore, we have often observed clinically that the symptoms of cerebral hemorrhage patients are more severe than those with cerebral infarctions; and they are also more damaging[8].

Research over several decades has shown that the obstruction of blood is the root cause of stroke occurring. In most stroke patients, pathological changes of microcirculation, hemodynamic disturbances, and hemorheologic modifications exist. As the main risk factors to atherosclerosis, hypertension, coronary heart disease and diabetes mellitus, the state of thick, viscous, agglomerates is very common in the blood circulation of patients[9,10].

(4) Qi deficiency

Qi deficiency refers to a morbid state in which the qi of the whole body is inadequate in quantity, and weakened in function. It is caused by an inadequate production of qi due to congenital deficiency, postnatal malnutrition, hypofunction of the lung, spleen and kidney, or by excessive consumption of qi due to overstrain, severe or prolonged illness. Its common clinical manifestations are fatigue, low spirits, spontaneous sweating, susceptibility to cold, dizziness and tinnitus, and a weak, or faint and thin pulse. Qi deficiency is an important cause of ischemic stroke. The activity of qi cannot circulate smoothly because of qi deficiency. When the uprising qi is insufficient, the blood circulation will be blocked, dizziness and headache will occur, and even an ischemic stroke can take place.

(5) Blood deficiency ♫

Blood is the red fluid circulating inside vessels with functions of nourishing and moistening, and also the basic material to form and sustain life activities. Compared with qi, blood pertains to yin, so it is also known as yin blood.

Blood mainly consists of nutritive qi and body fluids. Blood vessels are the passageways for blood circulation, so are known as blood houses. Blood circulates inside the whole body to nourish and moisten viscera, channels, body constituents, sense organs and orifices, to sustain life activities of the human body.

Vessels are the house for blood. Through vessels blood is distributed to the whole body.

Blood circulation is closely related to qi. The normal blood circulation depends on the qi's promoting, warming and consolidating functions. Through qi's promotion, blood can circulate endlessly; through qi's warming, blood can circulate fluently with warmth; through qi's consolidating, blood remains inside the vessels to avoid bleeding.

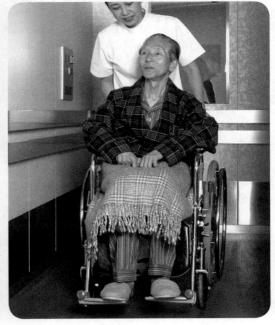

Blood circulation is the manifestation of the coordination among visceral functions. For example, the heart governs the blood vessels; sufficient heart qi can maintain a normal heart rate to promote blood circulation, so heart qi is a promoting force of blood circulation. The lung governs qi, assembles blood vessels and assists the heart to promote blood circulation, while the liver governs the smooth flow of qi to harmonize the qi activities of the whole body. The lung qi's dispersing, purifying and descending function and the liver qi's regulating flow of qi, are also major factors in promoting blood circulation. The spleen governs blood to keep blood inside the vessels, and the liver stores and regulates blood volume, both preventing bleeding.

From the above, normal blood circulation depends on the coordination of the functions of the heart, lung, spleen and liver; so disharmony in any one of these viscera can cause a disorder in the blood circulation. For example, deficient heart qi failing to promote, can result in blood circulation becoming obstructed; spleen qi deficiency can lead to blood leaking out the vessels, manifesting as bleeding diseases.

2. The Relationship between Qi and Blood

Qi pertains to yang, invisible and active, with functions of warming and promoting. Blood pertains to yin, visible and still, with functions of nourishing and moistening. Both depend on, and mutually promote, each other to sustain the life activities of the human body. The relationship between qi and blood are usually generalized as qi being the general of blood, and blood being the mother of qi. The former refers to qi's function on blood, and the latter refers to blood's function on qi.

(1)The effect of qi on blood

Functions of qi on blood include qi generating blood, qi circulating blood, and qi consolidating blood.

◆ Qi generating blood

It means that qi involves and promotes the production of blood; qi transformation is the promoting force for blood generation. For example, sufficient nutritive qi or visceral qi can generate sufficient blood due to vigorous qi transformation; otherwise deficient nutritive qi or visceral qi leads to hypofunction of qi transformation, manifesting as blood deficiency due to insufficient blood generation. Therefore in clinic, treatment for blood deficiency usually utilizes herbal prescriptions which tonify qi, because the qi will then generate blood.

◆ Qi circulating blood

Qi circulating blood means that qi can promote the blood circulating inside the vessels. Blood depends on the qi to circulate and distribute it throughout the whole body. For example, either qi deficiency failing to promote, or qi stagnation, can lead to a slowing of blood circulation resulting in blood stasis. Therefore, in clinical treatments for blood circulation disorders, herbal prescriptions to tonify qi, or circulate qi, are frequently used.

◆ Qi consolidating blood

Qi consolidating blood means that qi can consolidate blood to circulate inside the vessels to avoid bleeding. It mainly depends on the spleen qi governing blood i.e. the manifestation of qi's consolidating function in blood circulation. Spleen qi deficiency failing to consolidate blood, can lead to bleeding, manifesting as hematuria, hematochezia, and metrorrhagia.

(2) The effect of blood on qi

The two main effects of blood on qi, is blood generating qi, and blood transporting qi.

◆ Blood generating qi

It means that blood can supplement the qi of the human body. Physiological functions of viscera depend on promoting, warming and transforming of visceral qi. Blood circulates in the whole body to supplement nutrition to visceral qi,

to maintain it in a vigorous state. Therefore, sufficient blood ensures sufficient qi; otherwise deficient blood can lead to qi deficiency. In clinic, patients with chronic blood deficiency usually reflect qi deficiency too, and therefore the treatment should include tonifying qi and nourishing blood.

◆ Blood transporting qi

It means that qi is inside blood, and circulates the human body dependent upon blood. Blood is the vehicle of qi. Since qi is very vigorous and moves rapidly, it tends to disperse rather than assemble; it must depend on visible blood to circulate normally. In clinic, patients with severe bleeding usually have severe blood loss, manifesting in dangerous syndromes like qi collapse due to blood loss.

(3) Disharmony of qi and blood

Since qi and blood depend on each other, disharmony between them will inevitably lead to various pathological changes such as: qi stagnation and blood stasis; qi deficiency and blood stasis; failure of qi to control blood; deficiency of both qi and blood.

◆ Qi stagnation and blood stasis

This refers to a pathological state, in which an unregulated and depressed flow of qi makes the blood flow sluggish, thus resulting in qi stagnation and blood stasis.

It may result from emotional imbalances that make qi stagnant, or from traumatic injuries that damage the qi and blood. The clinical manifestations are fullness and pain in the chest and hypochondrium, petechia, ecchymosis, and abdominal mass.

◆ Qi deficiency and blood stasis

This refers to a pathological state in which insufficient qi fails to promote blood flow, resulting in the disturbance of blood flow, and leading to the concurrence of qi deficiency and blood stasis. It is usually caused by a longstanding illness, visceral weakness in the aged, and manifests as asthenic breathing, lack of strength, palpitations, chest pain, and a purple tongue.

◆ The failure of qi to control blood

This refers to a pathological state in which insufficient qi fails to keep the blood inside the vessels, consequently resulting in various symptoms of bleeding, such as hematochezia, hematuria, metrorrhagia, ecchymosis, and subcutaneous bleeding. It is the result of the impairment of the spleen qi due to prolonged illness failing to control blood.

◆ Deficiency of both qi and blood

This refers to a pathological condition characteristic of deficiency of both qi and blood. It is usually caused by consumption due to prolonged illness, or by loss of blood followed by depletion of qi, or by inadequate production of blood due to insufficient qi. It manifests clinically as pale or sallow complexion, asthenic breathing, reluctance to speak, lassitude and lack of strength, emaciation, palpitations, insomnia, dry skin and numbness in the extremities.

We can draw the conclusion that the disturbance of these four relationships of qi and blood will be the inducing factors, and pathological states of stroke. Harmonizing qi and blood is a significant principle in preventing and curing stroke.

3. Emotions

The seven emotions refer to seven emotional activities including joy, anger, worry, anxiety, sadness, fear and fright. They are external manifestations of the functional activities of viscera. Usually the seven emotions do not cause disease; only when the emotional stimulations are too abrupt, violent, prolonged and out of control, or when there is diminished adaptability due to imbalanced yin-yang, qi and blood of viscera, can they turn into pathogenic factors and cause disease. It is called "internal injury due to the seven emotions"[11].

Pathogenic characteristics of internal injury due to seven emotions:

Seven emotions correspond with the five *zang*. Strong emotional stimulation can affect qi movement of the viscera, resulting in various syndromes marked by disharmony of qi and blood[12].

(1) Rage leading to qi ascending

Rage impairs the liver, giving rise to an upward, adverse flow of liver qi. Clinical manifestations include red complexion and eyes, headache and dizziness, irritability, and susceptibility to rage. Bleeding due to the reverse flow of qi can result in hematemesis, and sudden coma. Transverse dysfunction of liver qi can result in gastric and abdominal pain, vomiting and diarrhea.

(2) Excessive joy leading to qi scattering

Sudden joy impairs the heart and results in slackened heart qi. In a mild cases, palpitations, fearful throbbings, asthenic breathing, weakness, and distractions will occur, and in a serious cases collapse of heart spirit will manifest as mental disorders and mania.

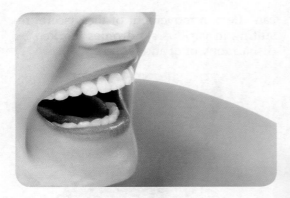

(3)Excessive sorrow leading to qi consumption

Excessive sorrow impairs the lungs, which results in an inability to disperse, purify and descend, and in the consumption of lung qi. Its clinical manifestations include asthenic breathing, reluctance to speak, chest oppression, bad temper and low spirits.

(4) Fear leading to qi sinking

Sudden and excessive fear impairs the kidney. Pathological changes of collapse of qi and insecurity of kidney qi will occur. Clinical manifestations include urine and fecal incontinence, spermatorrhea and prospermia.

(5) Fright leading to qi turbulence

Sudden fright impairs the heart and causes turbulence of the heart qi and abnormality of the heart-mind. Clinical manifestations include palpitations, restlessness, consternation, muteness, insomnia, susceptibility to fright, and even insanity.

(6) Pensiveness leading to qi knotting

Pensiveness or prolonged anxiety impairs the spleen, causing stagnation of spleen qi, failure of spleen in ascending, descending and inability of receiving and transforming. Clinical manifestations include poor appetite, abdominal distention, anorexia and loose stools.

(7) Worry leading to qi accumulation

Worry may lead to a blockage in the qi movement, manifesting as chest oppression, dysphoria, lassitude of limbs, sallow complexion, and lusterless hair.

Affecting the sequelae of diseases

Changes in the seven emotions can affect the onset, development, changes and sequelae of disease. Good spirits and optimism do not result in disease, but help patients recover. However, imbalances in the other emotions are apt to lead to disease and aggravate symptoms. For example, chest discomfort, and heart pain can be precipitated or aggravated by the seven emotions. The seven emotions can rapidly exacerbate malignant tumors. A good understanding of the seven emotions, and how they can affect diseases positively or negatively, can help doctors adopt a thorough and correct treatment method[13,14].

Stroke
Help From Chinese Medicine

Chapter 3

How Can a Healthy Body Be Maintained?

Stroke
Help From Chinese Medicine

A warning given by Sharon's stroke

December 18, 2005, Israeli Prime Minister Ariel Sharon suddenly suffered a minor stroke, and fell into a coma for a short period. During the evening of January 4, 2006, he suffered a serious stroke, causing a hemorrhage in large part of his brain. The hemorrhage was barely under control even after three surgeries, and his life was in grave danger. The whole world was shocked by his stroke. The media followed the events, creating discussions, and even the politicians commented on it. While the Israelis were concerned with his condition, the treatment and therapy he received also became a major topic. Why did Sharon's stroke provoke such a strong response?

Firstly, Sharon, the Prime Minister of Israel, was a very important figure in the Israeli and the Middle Eastern situation, which was of great significance to the whole world. Sharon had been in good health until he was suddenly hit by a stroke, and had to retire from the political stage. Politicians were concerned not only with the stability of the Middle East at this time, but also the effects of stroke threading human lives. This incident caused distress, and worry, especially among those political leaders who work hard all day and night, as they need to remain healthy in order to perform their important duties. There have been more than 10 important political leaders hit by stroke, and had to retire from work, or even lost their lives. These facts made those health workers and administrators realize the seriousness of stroke, and the necessity in preventing it from happening.

Secondly, ordinary people realized that if even the prime minister, who had a private doctor, could suffer a stroke and fall in a coma, then it was possible it could happen to them. The morbidity of cerebrovascular disease is approximately 200/100,000 per year, and is the second biggest killer of all diseases. There are 50%-80% of survivors who live with disabling sequelae such as hemiplegia, affected speech, mental deterioration, and even dementia. The relapse incidence within 5 years is 20%-47%, or even higher if blood pressure, cerebral arteriosclerosis and other predisposing factors are ignored. People pay special attention to stroke, because it is such a threat to human health and lives.

It's obvious that Sharon's living environment and medical cares were superior to others. He was in a good physical condition, as seen from TV and photographs. So what caused Sharon to suffer two strokes within three weeks of each other? This is what concerned the people the most. Although it might have looked like a random incident, something would have determined it; an unhealthy lifestyle and dietary habits, plus the ignorance of prevention, would have contributed to it.

These causes remind us that healthy lifestyles and avoiding bad habits are of great importance in curing and preventing stroke.

Diet

> Let food be your medicine and medicine be your food.
> -Hippocrates

Essentials of TCM Dietary Theory

According to the records of *Zhou Ceremony Chapter of Tian Guan*, China built the earliest medical system during the Zhou dynasty 3,000 years ago, where doctors were divided and defined into four types: the "dietician", the "physician", the "surgeon", and the "veterinarian", with the "dietician" thought to be most advanced. The "dietician" specialized in the diet of Emperor Zhou, similar to the modern clinical nutritionist. It is the earliest account of nutritional medicine practiced in the history of human, that we know.

The Yellow Emperor's Inner Classic from 2,000 years ago gives the following instructions for a proper diet, "The five grains are essential, the five fruits are beneficial, the five meats are helpful and the five vegetables supplement". This passage encourages a balanced diet. Grains, meat, fruit, and vegetables together supply nu-trients to support health. People need to consume a balanced variety of food.

Food therapy is the use of food for preventing and curing diseases, or promoting the rehabilitation of the diseased body. It is different from herbal therapy, and also from just an ordinary diet. One of the most significant features of food as a medicinal treatment is that it will cure disease and maintain a healthy body, with no toxic side effects on the human body. In other words, making use of certain characteristics and flavors of food from nature (meat, fruit and vegetables), which can be used for treatment or adjuvant therapy, to target specific syndromes. Adjusting yin and yang to achieve balance can contribute to the treatment of disease, and physical and psychological rehabilitation.

Food therapy involves treatment through food, which not only achieves physical health and prevents disease, but also provides enjoyment to the senses and spirit. This natural therapy is very different from taking the bitter herbal medicines. People find it easy to accept and follow food therapy long-term, and it is especially suitable for the treatment of chronic diseases. Regular meals should contain a wide variety of foods, with a balance of meat and vegetables, and snacks. Regular meals and a balanced diet are very important for maintaining good health.

Food performance refers to the nature and functions of food, which generate a significant basis of awareness and usage of food. The composition and different levels

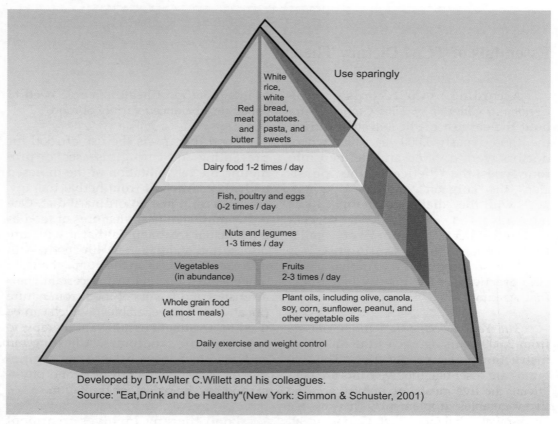

Developed by Dr.Walter C.Willett and his colleagues.
Source: "Eat,Drink and be Healthy"(New York: Simmon & Schuster, 2001)

Alternative Food Pyramid

of various food, create a variety of health effects in the human body. Understanding traditional Chinese medicine in relation to the diet includes the four natures and five tastes.

(1) Four natures and five tastes

Four natures relates to the temperature of foods: cold, hot, warm, and cool are the four natures; because cool is similar to cold, and warm is similar to hot in nature, they are actually two aspects of cold and heat. The nature of food is established due to the reaction caused when consuming the food. In general, foods of a cold nature have the effects of clearing heat-fire, suppressing hyperactive liver to calm the spirit, and relaxing the bowels. Cold foods such as watermelon, bitter gourd, radish, and pear, are mainly used in hot syndromes, with clinical manifestations of fever, thirst, distress, yellow urine, and constipation. Foods of a warm nature have the effects of warming the spleen and stomach for dispelling cold, suppressing hyperactive liver to calm the spirit, and increasing blood circulation to clear obstruction of the channels. Warm foods such as ginger, onions, garlic, pepper, and mutton, are suitable for cold syndromes, with clinical manifestations of aversion to cold, clear urine, and loose stools. Such food is appropriate for those with little resistance to cold. There are also neutral types of food, where the nature is neither cold nor warm, which stabilize the qi and blood, and invigorate the spleen to regulate the stomach. Regardless of whether there is a cold or hot syndrome, these foods can be used.

The five tastes refer to the acid, pungent, bitter, sweet, and salty tastes. The actual meaning of tastes are not just the concept of taste, but also contain the main content of function. Different tastes produce different effects. In general, sour, including astringency, stops sweating, diarrhea and seminal emissions. Reasonable consumption of sour foods, such as plums, is good for curing hyperhidrosis, long-term diarrhea, and spermatorrhea. Bitterness clears fire, and increases bowel movements. Bitter foods, such as bitter gourd, can be used in hot-disease fever, polydipsia, as well as other syndromes. The sweet taste nourishes and regulates the spleen and stomach, and relieves pain and spasms. Sweet foods, such as chestnuts, pumpkin, and jujube, can be used

for weak spleen and stomach, fatigue caused by deficiency of qi and blood, poor appetite, and abdominal pain. The pungent taste, including aromatic spicy taste, promotes sweating, activates qi, and improves appetite. Pungent foods such as onions, ginger, and pepper, are suitable for colds that produce aversion to cold, nasal congestion, runny nose, poor appetite, and stomach discomfort syndromes. The salty taste removes phlegm, and softens and resolves hard masses. Salty foods such as kelp, and seaweed, are useful for diseases caused by phlegm and blood obstruction, such as abdomen masses and other lumps. In addition, the acidity of vinegar, sweetness of sugar, pungency of spices, and saltiness of salt are also indispensable as seasonings, to enhance the appetite. Food can have one taste or be made up of a few different ones.

The following are some examples of common food items and their properties. A complete list of food properties is beyond the scope of this book. We hope that the list below will provide a good general outline, and help you make educated guesses about unlisted foods by comparing them to related items on the list.

Common Foods and Their Properties

Category	Hot	Warm	Neutral	Cold	Cool
Function	-Increase yang -Speed up qi -Warm up the body -These items tend to create heat and injure yin fluids	-Strengthen yang -Warm the qi and the organs	-Build up qi and body fluids -Stabilize and harmonize the body	-Cool internal heat -Calm down the spirit	-Slow down qi -Clear heat -Supplement body fluids
Beverages	Alcohol	-Cocoa -Coffee -Wine		Water	-Black tea -Fruit juices -Peppermint tea -Soy milk
Condiments			Honey	-Salt -Soy sauce	
Dairy		-Butter -Goat cheese	Cheese	Cow's milk	Yogurt
Animal products	Lamb	-Beef -Chicken -Eel -Salmon	-Carp -Duck -Egg -Pork -Goose	-Shrimp -Crayfish	Rabbit
Fruit and vegetables		-Cherry -Fennel -Leek -Peach -Onion	-Carrot -Cauliflower -Grape -Fig -Plum -Potato	-Asparagus -Banana -Orange -Rhubarb -Seaweed -Tomato -Watermelon	-Celery -Cucumber -Soy bean -Sprouts -Spinach -Zucchini

Category	Hot	Warm	Neutral	Cold	Cool
Grains and legumes			-Corn -Lentil -Millet -Peas -Rice -Spelt		-Barley -Tofu -Wheat
Herbs and spices	-Cinnamon -Chili -Curry -Garlic -Ginger -Paprika -Pepper	-Anise -Basil -Rosemary		-Dandelion -Yellow -Gentian	Tarragon
Nuts		Walnut	Hazelnut		

(The table is adapted from P23, Joweh Kastner. *Chinese Nutrition Therapy*. Thieme Stuttgart, New York, 2004)

Here are recommended vegetables, fruits, cereals, and meats suitable for stroke patients to eat. These foods contain the ingredients and nutrients, which are beneficial to patients with high risk factors for stroke, stroke patients, and patients of stroke sequelae. A correct and reasonable diet not only helps to prevent stroke, but is also beneficial for stroke rehabilitation.

◆ **Fruit**

Name: Apple
Property: cool
Taste: sweet
Special function: apple, rich in potassium, pectin, zinc, vitamin C, and flavonoids, can reduce blood pressure and lower lipid levels. Flavonoids are natural oxidants, which can inhibit oxidation of LDL. Pectin can lower concentrations of blood cholesterol, and prevent fat accumulation. High levels of zinc can enhance memory.

Name: Pear
Property: cool
Taste: sweet and slightly acidic
Special function: carbohydrate of pear is mainly fructose, which has little effect on postprandial blood glucose levels, so it is suitable for diabetic patients to eat. Recent studies have found that eating pear regularly is good for hypertension caused by liver yang, because pear can lower blood pressure, reduce lightheadedness and improve tinnitus and palpitations.

Name: Jujube
Property: plain
Taste: sweet
Special function: jujube contains rutin which strengthens blood vessels to lower blood pressure, and is used for hypertension prevention and treatment. It also nourishes to promote calmness, and is suitable for stroke sequelae patients with qi and blood deficiency, or insomnia.

Name: Kiwi fruit
Property: cold
Taste: sweet and acidic
Special function: kiwi fruit contains high quality dietary fiber, which promotes the excretion of cholesterol in feces to reduce blood cholesterol and triglycerides. It is the most beneficial fruit for hypertension, hyperlipidemia, and cerebrovascular disease.

Name: Apricot
Property: warm
Taste: sweet and acidic
Special function: apricot, rich in potassium, calcium, magnesium, flavonoids and polyphenols, lowers cholesterol and prevents high blood lipid levels. Regular consumption of dried apricots can improve blood circulation, fight infection, alleviate depression and insomnia, improve memory, enhance immunity, and assist in anti-aging.

Name: Dragon fruit
Property: plain
Taste: sweet
Special function: dragon fruit is high in fiber, and low in sugar and calories, so it is suitable for patients with diabetes, hypertension, and high cholesterol. The effects of anti-oxidation and anti-aging in Dragon fruit can inhibit the degeneration of brain cells and prevent dementia.

Name: Orange
Property: warm
Taste: pungent and slightly bitter
Special function: oranges contain hesperidin, citric acid, fructose, pectin, vitamin C and other nutrients, which increase the flexibility of capillaries, and prevent microvascular bleeding in the brain. It also has the effect of lowering blood cholesterol and controlling high blood pressure.

Name: Banana
Property: cold
Taste: sweet
Special function: tests show that potassium levels in bananas are higher than in all other fruits. Potassium is mainly distributed in the cells of the body, playing an important physiological role in the maintenance of neuromuscular excitability, maintaining normal systolic and diastolic functions of the heart, preventing arteriosclerosis, and protecting the cardiovascular system. Bananas also contain components to lower blood pressure. A large scale study of the American Heart Association was carried out on 4400 people aged 20 to 70, and confirmed that eating bananas long-term decreases the chance of stroke by 38%, compared with those that do not eat bananas. In addition, bananas relax the bowels and induce diuresis. When the elderly have to force stools due to constipation, blood pressure suddenly increases, which can cause stroke. Therefore by frequently eating bananas the elderly not only eliminate constipation, but also prevent the occurrence of stroke.

Dosage: 1-2 bananas per day
Note: diabetics should be careful as it has a high sugar content, which can be easily absorbed by the body.

Name: Olive
Property: plain
Taste: sweet, acidic, and slightly astringent
Special function: polyphenols have a strong antioxidant capacity. Olives also have the effect of relaxing muscles, lowering blood pressure, and preventing the occurrence of atherosclerosis. They are beneficial for complications of stroke. Olives and meat stew made into a drink, has the effect of relieving muscle rigidity and activating the collaterals affected in stroke, which is more beneficial for patients with hemiplegia.

Name: Lemon
Property: plain
Taste: sweet, and acidic
Special function: lemons contain citric acid, and are rich in vitamin C and vitamin P. They can help reduce blood pressure, and assist in adjuvant treatment of high blood lipids. Lemons contain a uniquely effective compound, the eriocitrin, which is not found in other fruits, and which can prevent the occurrence of organ dysfunction. Often lemon drinks can reduce the risk of high blood pressure, and the probability of myocardial infarction.

◆ **Vegetables**

Name: Onion
Property: warm
Taste: pungent
Special function: onions contain prostaglandins A, which expand blood vessels in order to relax blood vessels, lower blood viscosity, and reduce vascular pressure. Onions also contain diallyl disulfide, and sulfur-containing amino acids, which enhance the activity of fibrinolysis, lower lipid levels, and prevent atherosclerosis.

Note: Honey and onions conflict with each other; eating them together can cause bloating.

Name: Cucumber
Property: cold
Taste: sweet
Special function: it is reported that cucumbers contain alcohol acid, which although can inhibit sugars turning into fat in the body, also hinders sugars providing energy to the body. In addition, cucumbers lower cholesterol levels. Often cucumbers are beneficial for patients with hypertension, hyperlipidemia, and obesity, and they help prevent the occurrence of atherosclerosis and stroke.

Name: Tomato
Property: slightly cold
Taste: sweet, and acidic
Special function: niacin contained in tomatoes can promote the formation of red blood cells, maintain the flexibility of blood vessel walls, and protect the skin. Eating tomatoes is beneficial for the prevention and treatment of atherosclerosis, hypertension and stroke. Tomatoes contain dietary fiber and prevent constipation. A new study in London found that lycopene, an antioxidant extracted from the tomato, can prevent stroke and heart disease.

Name: Black fungus
Property: plain
Taste: sweet
Special function: modern research found that the nucleic acid in black fungus can significantly reduce blood cholesterol levels. The high-cellulose contained in it can promote intestinal excretion of cholesterol, and have a positive effect in controlling high blood cholesterol. Black fungus contains high levels of adenosine, which can be effective in anti-platelet aggregation, in reducing blood clotting, preventing thrombosis, and preventing stroke and atherosclerosis. Research has shown that if you eat 10-15 g of black fungus every day, its effects on the anti-platelet aggregation compares with that of a low dose aspirin a day. To elderly with constipation can prevent cancer, aging, and a variety of age-related diseases, by eating black fungus, or fungus porridge.

Name: Carrot
Property: plain
Taste: sweet
Special function: some studies show that those who eat a carrot every day have significantly reduced risk of stroke compared with those who do not eat carrots. This is mainly due to β-carotene which can be converted into vitamin A, to prevent the accumulation of cholesterol in the blood vessel walls, maintaining cerebrovascular flow and thus preventing stroke. Carrots also contain higher levels of cellulose and pectin calcium, which can reduce cholesterol, preventing coronary artery disease and stroke.

Note: Carrots are fat soluble, and are best cooked with meat.

Name: Garlic
Property: warm
Taste: pungent
Special function: modern pharmacology proves that allicin contained in garlic, is anti-inflammatory, reduces blood lipids, and reduces some of the pharmacological effects of thrombosis:

> Reduces cholesterol crystals, reduces blood lipids.
> Effective resistance to calcium deposits, reduces peripheral vascular resistance, lowers blood pressure.
> Softens the blood vessels, prevents blood vessel atherosclerosis, prevents blood vessel rupture.

> Prevents thrombosis and reduces the incidence of myocardial infarction and cerebral embolism.

Name: Spinach
Property: cold
Taste: sweet
Special function: spinach leaves contain chromium, and an insulin-like substance that can stabilize blood sugar. Spinach contains many anti-oxidants such as vitamin E and selenium, which promote anti-aging and the proliferation of cells. These activate the brain, to prevent the brain from aging, and are effective in the prevention and treatment of Alzheimer's disease. Studies have shown that women who eat one serving of spinach every day reduce their risk of stroke by 35% more than those who eat one serving a month.

Note: spinach should be boiled up in water first, because it contains much oxalic acid, which will hinder the body's absorption of calcium.

Name: Mushroom
Property: plain
Taste: sweet
Special function: mushrooms contain heterogeneous proteins. Modern medical studies have shown that they digest fat, lower blood pressure, and are very effective in the treatment and prevention of stroke, especially in those patients with high blood lipids and unstable blood pressure. Mushroom polysaccharides can enhance the activity of T cells, which boosts the immune function. Clinical observation shows that patients with hyperlipidemia can reduce their lipid levels by eating 90 g fresh mushrooms fried in a small amount of vegetable oil, or 90 g fresh mushroom soup.

Name: Yam
Property: plain
Taste: sweet
Special function: regular consumption of yams increases the mucus proteins in the body. For example, the polysaccharide protein prevents fat deposits in the cardiovascular system, maintains the elasticity of blood vessels, and prevents the premature occurrence of atherosclerosis. Dopamine in yam dilates blood vessels and improves the blood circulation. In addition, yam also improves the digestive function, and enhances physical fitness.

Name: Potato
Property: cool
Taste: sweet
Special function: potato, rich in B vitamins and fiber, has an important role in delaying the aging process, and controlling blood cholesterol levels. It contains potassium, which can prevent the rupturing of cerebral blood vessels and reduces the risk of stroke. Some scholars have reported that eating a potato a day decreases the chance of stroke by 40%.

Name: Pumpkin
Property: warm
Taste: sweet
Special function: pumpkin is rich in cobal which actives the body's metabolism, promotes hematopoietic function, and participates in the synthesis of vitamin B12, which is an essential trace elements in the pancreatic islet cells. It also prevents and treats diabetes, and lowers blood sugars. It is a suitable food for stroke patients with diabetes mellitus.

Name: Celery
Property: cool
Taste: sweet and bitter
Special function: studies of modern medicine suggest that celery is full of crude fiber, and is rich in minerals, vitamins, mannitol, and volatile oil. It also contains materials that can reduce blood pressure, lower lipid levels, and assist the break down of fat, thereby facilitating the treatment of hypertension, hyperlipidemia and obesity, and can be used in diet therapy for multi-phase stroke.

◆ Legume, cereal, nut

Name: Tofu
Property: cool
Taste: sweet and tasteless
Special function: tofu is full of nutrients, essential trace elements, and a high quality protein known as "plant meat". Two small pieces of tofu contain a person's daily requirements of calcium. Tofu is the recommended food for patients with high blood pressure, high blood fat, high cholesterol and arteriosclerosis, and coronary heart disease, because it is cholesterol free. Tofu is rich in soy lecithin, which benefits nerves, blood vessels, brain growth and development, and is useful in the after care of stroke patients.
Note: tofu contains purines, so gout patients should be cautious. Over eating tofu may cause abdominal distention and nausea; this may be resolved by eating pineapple.

Name: Green bean
Property: cool
Taste: sweet and tasteless
Special function: mung beans are the best food to clear and nourish. Stroke patients can eat green beans to suppress hyperactive liver yang, to reduce irritable moods, and to lower blood pressure, which are all conducive to recovery.

Name: Buckwheat
Property: plain
Taste: sweet
Special function: niacin, contained in buckwheat, promotes the body's metabolism, enhances the detoxification capacity, expands small blood vessels, and lowers blood cholesterol. Buckwheat is rich in vitamin P (rutin), which is an anti-oxidant that softens the capillaries, stabilizes blood pressure, and prevents cerebral hemorrhage. Buckwheat also has the capacity to stimulate brain function, extending the life of brain cells.

Name: Corn
Property: plain
Taste: sweet
Special function: corn oil contains unsaturated fatty acids, calcium, and vitamin E, which regulates the normal metabolism of cholesterol, and reduces blood lipid levels. Long-term consumption can lower blood pressure and blood sugar, helping to control the occurrence of stroke. Recently, a study from the German Association of Nutrition and Healthcare showed that corn's nutritional value and health benefits are the highest among all staple foods. Corn can also stimulate the brain cells, and enhance brain power and memory function.

Name: Oats
Property: plain
Taste: sweet
Function: nourishes deficiency to alleviate sweating.

Special function: oats are rich in linoleic acid and vitamin E, and reduce serum total cholesterol (TC) and triglycerides (TG). Simultaneously they protect the brain cells, slow the cellular aging process, and prevent stroke. According to the report of a 12 year study in the United States, consumption of a large number of whole grains foods can significantly reduce the risk of suffering a stroke.

Name: Walnut
Property: warm
Taste: sweet
Special function: walnuts contain protein and unsaturated fatty acids essential to human nutrition, which are important for brain tissue metabolism; nourishing brain cells and enhancing brain function. Walnuts can reduce the absorption of intestinal cholesterol, to exclude "impurities" from the blood vessel wall. Purifying the blood enables fresh blood to circulate through the body. Therefore, walnuts prevent atherosclerosis, and lower cholesterol. Walnuts, rich in saturated fatty acids linoleic acid and linolenic acid, benefit the brain and nerves, preventing arteriosclerosis and frequent constipation. Walnuts are most effective for stroke patients with anxiety, insomnia, memory loss, and constipation, and can be utilized as an adjuvant therapy for hemiplegia and dementia after stroke.

Note: Walnut is greasy, so patients with diarrhea should be cautious.

◆ Diary products

Name: Milk
Property: warm
Taste: sweet
Special function: milk is rich in calcium, protein, and fat. When calcium in milk is combined with protein, they are both very easily absorbed by the body. Drinking milk can delay aging, prevent disease, and enhance physical fitness. Chinese medical science believes that milk can nourish the spleen and stomach to benefit the qi. Stroke patients with hemiplegia, distorted mouth and dysphagia, have some difficulty in feeding; drinking milk or nasal feeding may be helpful for the physical rehabilitation of stroke patients.

◆ Seafood and meat

Name: Carp
Property: plain
Taste: sweet
Special function: carp meat is rich in potassium; 334 mg potassium per 100 g carp. It prevents hypokalemia, and increases muscle strength, which is consistent with TCM's theory of "spleen rules the muscles and limbs". Its head is rich in lecithin, which maintains brain nutrition, and enhances memory. Carp contains mostly unsaturated fatty acids, which can reduce cholesterol and prevent arteriosclerosis and stroke.

Name: Beef
Property: warm
Taste: sweet
Special Function for stroke: beef is rich in proteins, and its amino acid composition is closer to human's requirements than pork. It can improve the body's resistance to disease, strengthen recovery post-operatively, and fortify recovery after blood loss and tissue repair.

Name: Chicken
Property: plain
Taste: sweet
Special function: chicken contains unsaturated fatty acids, oleic acid (mono-unsaturated fatty acids) and linoleic acid (polyunsaturated fatty acids), which reduce the level of low-density lipoprotein cholesterol which is harmful to the body. Chicken is very therapeutic to counter-act after-stroke malnutrition, with aversion to cold, fatigue, and weakness. The wing meat is rich in bone collagen, which strengthens blood vessels, muscles and tendons.

Note: gout patients should avoid chicken soup, due to its high content of purines, which aggravate the disease.

(2) Specifics and Recipes

◆ Porridges

The following rice porridges can be eaten every day to help preventing stroke. While some of the ingredients are medicinal substances, their effect is mild with the given dosages, and will not cause any side affects. They work slowly over an extended period. Because of this, the recipes given here are safe to eat and drink every day.

Garlic barley porridge

Ingredients: rice 40 g, oats 40 g, barley 40 g, garlic 30 g, leek 10 g, Chinese wolfberries 3 g.

Method: soak rice, oats, and barley for 6 hours. Place rice, oats, barley, and peeled garlic into a pot, cover with water and simmer over low heat for 2 hours. Then turn off the heat, add some Chinese wolfberries, and thin slices of garlic.

Effects: lowers cholesterol, prevents blood clots and occurrence of strokes.

Mung bean porridge

Ingredients: rice 50 g, green beans 50 g; add together to make porridge.

Method: soak for 2 hours, cover with water and simmer over low heat till it turns soft.

Effects: mung beans lower lipid levels in diabetic patients with hypertension or coronary heart disease, but is not suitable for diabetic patients with kidney disease.

Spinach porridge

Ingredients: spinach 100-150 g, rice 50 g.

Method: soak rice for 1 hour, heating rice in boiling water till it turns soft, then add slices of spinach, and turn off the heat, add little salt, eat every morning and evening.

Yam porridge

Ingredients: Chinese yam 60 g, rice 60 g.

Method: soak rice for 1 hour, boiling in the water for 30 minutes, then make the yam into a paste. Fry some honey and butter together until condensed, and then crumble to bits with a spoon and put into the porridge.

◆ **Tea**

Tea is not only a beverage, but can also have a medicinal effect of strengthening the health.

Green tea

Green tea contains anti-oxidants that can help to combat aging. Catechins in green tea can significantly increase SOD (Superoxide Dismutase) activity, and clear free radicals. Studies have shown that tea polyphenols can remove harmful excess free radicals in the body, and regenerate α-VE, VC, GSH, SOD and other antioxidant substances of the body. This protects and repairs the anti-oxidation system, which is useful in enhancing the body's immunity, and protecting the body against the effects of cancer and aging. Long-term drinking of green tea can lower blood sugar, blood lipids, and blood pressure, thus preventing cerebrovascular disease. Animal experiments indicate that the catechins in tea can lower total cholesterol, free cholesterol, low-density lipoprotein cholesterol, and triglyceride in plasma, while increasing high-density lipoprotein cholesterol. Experiments on the human body show that it could inhibit platelet aggregation and reduce the incidence of atherosclerosis. Green tea contains flavonols, an antioxidant, which may also prevent blood clots and platelet clumps, reducing cerebrovascular disease.

Fiveleaf gynostemma herb

Gynostemma can lower fat and cholesterol, enhance the coronary and cerebral blood flow, improve immune function, and be effective in the prevention and treatment of atherosclerosis. It is beneficial for patients with atherosclerosis, high blood pressure, and high cholesterol

to drink this tea. In recent years, scientists have found that the content of four kinds of saponin in Gynostemma is greater than in ginseng, and it that it has a significant effect to benefit the qi and lower blood sugar, as it supports glucose metabolism. Gynostemma is suitable for serving alone, and should not be taken with other teas.

Preparation: gently steep 1 tsp dried Gynostemma in a cup of boiling water for 10 minutes, then add rock sugar or honey as desired, before drinking.

Cassia seed peach kernel tea

Ingredients: peach kernel 10 g, cassia seed 30 g.

Function: the tea suppresses hyperactive liver and clears heat, promotes blood circulation and relaxes the bowels; it is most suitable for stroke patients with cerebral thrombosis who have constipation.

Sanchi tea

Ingredients: sanchi 3 g, green tea 3 g.

Preparation: wash sanchi, then dry by sunlight or heat; cut into slices, or grind into a powder, then add to the green tea and boiling water. Cover and brew for 15 minutes before serving.

Functions: activates blood circulation. Applicable to use where fatty liver is

due to qi stagnation, and blood stasis. Dosage: Continuously brew the tea 3-5 times, and drink frequently throughout the day. Once the tea is finished the Sanchi pieces can be chewed.

(3) Recipes for different patterns

Sun Si-miao

Sun Si-miao, a famous doctor of the *Tang* Dynasty (618-907 A.D.), said that when a person fell sick, the physician should first regulate the patient's diet and lifestyle. In many conditions, these changes alone are enough to affect a cure over time. Sun Si-miao said that only if diet and lifestyle changes are not enough should the physician administer other treatments, such as herbs or acupuncture. Most patients seeking professional treatment from Chinese medicine need herbs and/or acupuncture, as well as changes to their diet and lifestyle, in order to bring about a cure. Without appropriate changes in diet and lifestyle, treatment with herbs and acupuncture cannot achieve a full and lasting effect.

A medicinal diet is simply food therapy prescribed according to the theories of Chinese medicine, and aimed at treatment of disease and health cultivation. In Chinese medicine many foods are used as herbs, and likewise many herbs are eaten as food. Using a medicinal diet allows a treatment to be more comprehensive, as with every meal a patient is consuming substances that help bring the body closer to balance.

TCM esteems that food is better than drugs; so food has been used as medicine instead. It is a form of unique healthcare therapy for both prevention and treatment, and suitable for stroke patients. Diet for stroke patients is based on the cause of the stroke, and the patient's symptoms, which can be divided into four main groups:

◆ **Supplement qi and activate blood circulation**

Pale body, weight loss, spontaneous sweating, fatigue, skin numbness, or partial body numbness, scaly dry skin, ecchymosis petechia on tongue or dark tongue, and a thin and astringent pulse. Chinese medicine diet therapy is often used to benefit qi and activate blood circulation.

Medicinals That Can Be Used in Cooking

Chinese Name	Common Name	Pinyin	Latin Name
黄芪	astragalus root	*huáng qí*	Radix Astragali
地龙	earth worm	*dì lóng*	Pheretima
桃仁	peach seed	*táo rén*	Semen Persicae
当归	Chinese angelica	*dāng guī*	Radix Angelicae Sinensis
川芎	chuanxiong root	*chuān xiōng*	Rhizoma Chuanxiong
红花	safflower	*hóng huā*	Flos Carthami
赤芍	red peony root	*chì sháo*	Radix Paeoniae Rubra
党参	codonopsis root	*dǎng shēn*	Radix Codonopsis
三七	notoginseng root	*sān qī*	Radix et Rhizoma Notoginseng
丹参	danshen root	*dān shēn*	Radix et Rhizoma Salviae Miltiorrhizae

Recommended recipes:

Guī shēn shàn yú tāng (**Chinese angelica, codonopsis root and mud eel soup**)

Ingredients: codonopsis root 15 g, Chinese angelica 15 g, eel 500 g.

Preparation: clean the eel, then cut into pieces; add cooking wine, soy sauce, green onion, and ginger, and then boil them with a muslin bag containing codonopsis root and Chinese angelica. Remove any foam as it simmers on a low heat for 1 hour. Remove the muslin bag, adding sesame oil and other spices.

Function: benefits qi and activates circulation, removes obstruction in the collaterals.

Dosage: 1 dose every 1-2 days for 15 days. Eat the fish and drink soup.

◆ **Nourish liver and kidney and benefit yin**

Hemiplegia, fatigue, tinnitus, forgetfulness, blurred vision, difficulty in extension and contraction, sluggish, mental fatigue, pale complexion, unresponsive, weak feet, nocturnal enuresis, poor urination, dry mouth with thirst, dream disturbed sleep, red tongue with thin coat, and a thin string pulse.

Medicinals That Can Be Used in Cooking

Chinese Name	Common Name	Pinyin	Latin Name
山药	common yam rhizome	*shān yào*	Rhizoma Dioscoreae
枸杞子	Chinese wolfberry fruit	*gǒu qǐ zǐ*	Fructus Lycii
龟板	Tortoise plastron	*guī bǎn*	Plastrum Testudinis
杜仲	eucommia bark	*dù zhòng*	Cortex Eucommiae
牛膝	two-toothed achyranthes root	*niú xī*	Radix Achyranthis Bidentatae
熟地黄	prepared rehmannia root	*shú dì huáng*	Radix Rehmanniae Praeparata
山茱萸	cornus	*shān zhū yú*	Fructus Corni
麦冬	dwarf lilyturf tuber	*mài dōng*	Radix Ophiopogonis
益智仁	sharp leaf glangal fruit	*yì zhì rén*	Fructus Alpiniae Oxyphyllae

Recommended recipes:

Dù zhòng niú xī zhū jí tāng (Eucommia, achyranthes and pig spine soup)

Ingredients: eucommia bark 30 g, two-toothed achyranthes root 15 g, pork spine 500 g, Chinese dates 5 g.

Preparation: rinse pork chop and break the spine; use boiling water to boil off the blood, and then add eucommia, achyranthes, red dates (remove stones) altogether in the pot with water to cover. Bring to boil on a high heat, and then simmer for 2-3 hours; add seasoning to serve.

Function: benefits the kidney, tendons and bones.

Huái qǐ jiǎ yú tāng (Chinese yam, wolfberry fruit and turtle soup)

Ingredients: Chinese yam 30 g, wolf-

berry fruit 15 g, a soft-shelled turtle (about 300 g), 2 pieces of ginger, wine 1 tsp, a little salt.

Preparation: wash Chinese yam and the medlar. Remove the membrane and internal organs of the soft-shelled turtle, and then place into a pan with the Chinese yam, medlar, ginger and wine. Cover with water and bring to boil on a high heat; stew on low heat for 2-3 hours, then add a little salt for seasoning, before drinking the soup and eating the meat.

◆ **Nourish spleen to remove phlegm**

Limp with weakness, insensitivity, loss of appetite, malaise and fatigue, overweight, pale lips and yellow face, puffy tongue with scallops or pale tongue with greasy coat, and a thin and slippery pulse.

Medicinals That Can Be Used in Cooking

Chinese Name	Common Name	Pinyin	Latin Name
薏苡仁	coix seed	*yì yǐ rén*	Semen Coicis
薤白	long stamen onion bulb	*xiè bái*	Bulbus Allii Macrostemi
白术	white atractylodes rhizome;	*bái zhú*	Rhizoma Atractylodis Macro-cephalae
人参	ginseng	*rén shēn*	Radix et Rhizoma Ginseng
陈皮	aged tangerine peel	*chén pí*	Pericarpium Citri Reticulatae
瓜蒌	snakegourd fruit	*guā lóu*	Fructus Trichosanthis
竹沥	bamboo sap	*zhú lì*	Succus Bambusae
半夏	pinellia rhizome	*bàn xià*	Rhizoma Pinelliae
茯苓	Indian bread	*fú líng*	Poria

Recommended recipes:

Jú pí shān zhā zhōu **(Orange peel and hawthorn porridge)**

Ingredients: orange peel 10 g, hawthorn berry (dried) 15 g, radish seed 12 g, glutinous rice 100 g.

Preparation: dry the ingredients separately, then crush into a powder. Boil rice into porridge, adding the powder when almost ready, plus a pinch of salt for seasoning. Eat warm. Suitable for those with high blood lipids.

Yì dòu luó bo zhōu **(Coix seed, white kidney bean and white radish porridge)**

Ingredients: coix seed 30 g, white kidney beans 30 g, Chinese yam 30 g, white radish 60 g, rice 60 g.

Preparation: peel and dice fresh yam and cut radish into pieces. Add coix seeds, white beans, and rice into water and boil for 10 minutes until it turns to porridge.

Add the yam and white radish into the thick porridge.

Function: benefits the spleen to remove dampness.

Dosage: once a day, for 7-10 days.

◆ **Suppress hyperactive liver to descend yang and calm endogenous wind**

Dizziness and tinnitus, head pain, red eyes, irritability, palpitations and forgetfulness, insomnia and dream disturbed sleep, large upper body, flat feet, a strong and stringy or a stringy, thready and rapid pulse.

Medicinals That Can Be Used in Cooking

Chinese Name	Common Name	Pinyin	Latin Name
天麻	tall gastrodis tuber	*tiān má*	Rhizoma Gastrodiae
钩藤	gambir plant	*gōu téng*	Ramulus Uncariae Cum Uncis
珍珠母	mother-of-pearl	*zhēn zhū mǔ*	Concha Margaritiferae Usta
牡蛎	oyster shell	*mǔ lì*	Concha Ostreae
决明子	sea-ear shell	*jué míng zǐ*	Concha Haliotidis
僵蚕	stiff silkworm	*jiāng cán*	Bombyx Batryticatus
全蝎	scorpion	*quán xiē*	Scorpio
水蛭	leech	*shuǐ zhì*	Hirudo

Recommended recipes:

Jué míng hǎi dài tāng (**Cassia seed and seaweed soup**)

Ingredients: seaweed 30 g, cassia seed 15 g, pork 150 g, pinch of salt.

Preparation: wash the seaweed, cut into pieces and soak. Rinse the pork and

cassia seeds, cutting the pork into pieces, and then place all the ingredients into a pot. Cover with water and simmer for 2 hours, filter the dregs, add a pinch of salt, and eat.

Zhēn zhū mǔ lì zhōu (Mother-of-pearl and oyster porridge)

Ingredients: mother-of-pearl powder 5 g, oyster 50 g, rice 100 g.
Preparation: boil mother-of-pearl powder and oysters with 500 ml water; filter out the dregs, and then add rice to make porridge.
Dosage: twice a day.

(4) Foods to avoid for stroke patients

Stroke can be divided into different phases dependent upon the course of the disease: precursor of stroke, stroke, and stroke sequelae. In the different phases there are certain foods that should be avoided.

◆ Precursor of stroke phase

In the precursor of stroke phase, with symptoms such as dizziness and numbness, greasy food and alcohol in particular should be avoided. Light and easily digestible foods, mainly vegetables and fruits, should be eaten[15].

◆ Stroke phase

At this stage, if the patient is groggy or in a coma, all consumption should be avoided temporarily, until the critical stage has passed. If the patient remains unconscious, they can be given nasal feeding liquid. Conscious patients can have a liquid, or semi-liquid diet, such as milk, soup, or pork soup boiled with thin rice gruel. In the recovery process, it is recommended to eat congee (rice soup), vegetable and fruit juices, and to avoid spicy foods, such as onions, garlic, pepper, roast goose, roast duck and so on. Foods that replenish the qi and blood, nourish the liver and kidney, and are more nutritious, can also be eaten in moderate consumption, such as eggs, lean meat, fish, fresh vegetables and fruit. However, greasy, fatty foods, alcohol and smoking must be avoided during this phase[16].

◆ **Stroke sequelae phase**

Sequelae of stroke generally refers to the period six months and onwards, after the stroke. During this time, the diet is also extremely important to the patient's health, both to promote recovery as soon as possible, and also to prevent further strokes. In general less animal fat should

be eaten; a low-fat diet should be encouraged, using more vegetable oil, because vegetable oil contains more vitamin E and is rich in unsaturated fatty acids, which can reduce blood cholesterol and the hardening of the arteries, to prevent further strokes. Animal's internal organs such as heart, intestines, and brain, as well as egg yolk, roe, shellfish and other high cholesterol-containing foods, should be eaten less frequently[17].

Multi-paralyzed patients are mostly restricted to long-term bed rest or a decline in activity, leading to poor digestion and absorption, and resulting in constipation; a conditioning diet is preferable. Nutritious, easily digestible foods such as dairy, fish, chicken, eggs, and soybean products are recommended. To counteract constipation, whole grains, celery, edible fungus, and honey can be eaten. Foods rich in B vitamins, such as bananas, apples, eggs, and soy products should also be eaten, as these are conducive to nerve repair and stroke recovery[18,19].

Exercises

1. What Exercises Are Helpful and What Should Be Avoided?

Because of the variety of locations affected and the extent of damage produced, many different symptoms can be observed in stroke patients. Paralysis of the limbs is the most common, and it is still the highest factor in affecting the quality of patients' lives. Therefore the primary task of rehabilitation therapy is to restore, or improve limb paralysis after a stroke. The manifestation of movement disorders after strokes can be summed up in the three following aspects: dystonia, muscle paralysis, and selective movement loss. Muscle paralysis is the most characteristic symptom of stroke patients. Although the distribution of dystonia can be spread in the upper and lower limbs, the typical pattern is curving in the upper limbs, and stretching in the lower limbs, while the loss of selective movement is manifested as inflexibility, uncoordination, and dysfunction[20].

(1)The importance of immediate exercise for rehabilitation after stroke

Early stage rehabilitation training can concentrate on the following: stimulating various neurons on the moving path, regulating their excitability, and stimulating parts of the brain cells to produce functional compensation. By focusing on these, new contacts in the nervous system can be established as soon as possible, in order to regain the correct motor output and promote substantial rehabilitation[21]. Simultaneously, exercise initiated early on, can prevent limb contractures, reduce orthostatic hypotension, and prevent and reduce osteoporosis, pressure sores, pulmonary infection, urinary tract infections and other complications, as well as shorten hospital stays. The earlier rehabilitation training begins, the greater the possibility of functional recovery, and a better prognosis. Therefore, it is important that the rehabilitation training begins as soon as possible[22].

(2)Exercise with the guidance of Chinese medicine

In the theory of Chinese medicine, exercise enhances physical strength, strengthens bones, increases muscle flexibility, regulates cholestasis, harmonizes the qi and blood, and balances the yin, yang, qi and blood in the organs. In Chinese medicine there is a saying "Only when yin is calm and yang is sound, can the spirit be in equilibrium".

Chinese medicine believes that stroke is related to old age, a weak body, and liver and kidney deficiency. A lifespan of 100 years originates from healthy feet; the old saying goes "Just as a dry tree begins to die from the roots up, so a person's health deteriorates from the feet up".

"To keep fit and healthy, put your feet in warm water every night before going to sleep. With this method it will be unnecessary to take any medicine". Press acupoints on the feet, for example, KI 1 (*yǒng quán*, 涌泉), KI 3 (*tài xī*, 太溪), and acupoints on the arm and hand, such as, LI 4 (*hé gǔ*, 合谷), LI 11 (*qū chí*, 曲池), for 1-2 minutes each point, daily. The effects of these will clear liver heat and drain fire, and enrich and nourish kidney yin.

kidney. The most effective method is to use the thumb and index finger to pinch the 10 toes, to use the index and middle fingers to clamp and pinch the fingers of left hand pulling down to the fingertips, and to use the left fingers to pinch the right fingertips.

Hand washing is also a beneficial technique; first wash your hands with cold water, and then with hot water. Chinese medicine believes that the three yang channels and three yin channels cross at the hands. The cold and hot stimulation affects the cerebral blood vessels, and can prevent further strokes.

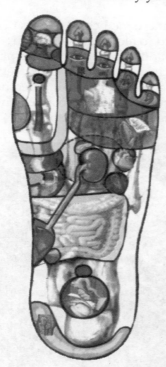

Exercising fingers and toes is beneficial to enhance peripheral circulation, and increase blood flow to the heart, brain and

The human body is full of meridian points, with the neck being the interchange of meridian collaterals. The hands, feet, ears, head, face and other parts, are full of holographic reflex areas of the organs. Regularly exercising and massaging these areas can relax tendons and increase blood circulation, removing any blockages from the meridian pathways. Exercising these areas is very simple and efficient, and regular practice can prevent serious illnesses, including stroke[23].

◆ Use your left hand

A new study reported that people, especially the elderly, should learn to use their left hand; this can prevent a stroke from occurring. More than 90% of the population is right-handed, therefore the left side of the brain receives more exercise, while the right side of the brain rarely receives any. The right cerebral blood vessels become more fragile due to limited use, and therefore the possibility of rupture,

which induces stroke, is much greater. Therefore the right-handed person, especially the elderly, should begin to use their left hand more frequently; this will improve the blood vessels and functions of right brain. Similarly, the left handed person should begin to use their right hand more frequently to increase their skill, and the activity in their left brain.

◆ Clench your teeth together

Clench the upper and lower teeth together tightly, and then open and close many times. Increase your vigor when tightly clenching the teeth, and do not separate the teeth when relaxing the jaw. This contracts and dilates the blood vessels, the head and neck muscles, and the scalp and face, accelerating the blood flow in the cerebral blood vessels, restoring the flexibility of the cerebral blood vessels which are gradually developing into cirrhosis, and adequately supplying blood and oxygen to the brain. Doing this will decrease, and may even eliminate the chance of stroke[24].

◆ Turn your head

Professors discovered that there is a low incidence of stroke in painters, and related it to the fact of their heads moving up and down whilst working. The rolling movement in different directions can decrease the pressure in cerebral blood vessels, which helps to prevent a stroke. The recommended technique is: sit and allow the neck muscles to relax, and then fully extend your neck by slowly turning your head to the left and then the right, 30-50 times, daily.

◆ Shrug

Shrugging can relax the nerves, blood vessels and muscles, which increases the blood circulation to remove any blockages in the channels, and increases the blood flow from the carotid artery to the brain. The recommended technique is: lifting the shoulders up and then relaxing down, repeatedly, for 6 minutes daily.

◆ Rub your neck

Stroke is related to atherosclerotic plaques, which are of deposits of cholesterol building up on the carotid artery. Regularly rubbing the neck can prevent the occurrence of a stroke, because it promotes the smooth, vascular muscles to relax, improves the nutrition of the blood vessel walls, softens the sclerous blood vessels in the neck, restores flexibility and improves the blood supply to the brain. The recommended technique is: rubbing the hands together until heated, and then massaging both sides of the neck quite fast, using moderate strength, until the neck feels hot and red. Carry out daily, for 6 minutes every morning and evening.

(3)Important tips in rehabilitation

Planned rehabilitation exercise cannot only reduce the mortality and recurrence rate of strokes, but also improves the circulation through the blood vessels. This reduces the risk of thrombosis, and enhances the efficiency and storage capacity of the cardio-cerebral vascular system. Nevertheless, it could be detrimental to blindly follow unscientific exercises which may harm one's health. Some important points to be aware of during rehabilitation:

➤ Start with a small amount of exercise, and gradually increase, remembering to put safety first. Begin to increase joint flexibility, and then progress to low intensity movement. Over time steadily increase the exercise intensity and duration, dependent upon each individual's condition.

➤ Keep the movement safe, avoiding high impact or jarring movements. Be conscious of what the body is capable of, and do not over exert. Exercise appropriately, without straining the heart.

➤ Adopt the training method of low intensity movements over a long period, resting well, and gradually increasing in intensity over time.

➤ Pay more attention to the body, and become more aware of any changes, specifically to the heart rate.

➤ Pay attention to changes in environmental conditions. It is very common in the elderly, for poor blood circulation to affect the ability to sweat, and therefore regulate body temperature. If the environment is not suitable for exercise (for example, excessive heat or very cold weather, low air pressure and humidity, or poor ventilation), then the intensity of movement should be appropriately reduced.

2. Qi Gong , Tai Ji Quan and *Bā Duàn Jǐn*

(1) Qi Gong ♄

Qi gong and physical activity play an important role in regulating the autonomic nervous system, and reducing the over stimulation of the adrenal glands. Qi gong, especially relaxing qi gong is suggested. Standing qi gong, strengthening qi gong and moving qi gong can also be considered, dependent upon individual conditions. Imagination and simple movements are required when doing qi gong; it is useful to focus on a place below the

heart, such as the *dān tián* or KI 1. Qi gong practice, whether still or moving, all share the common principles that underliepin the theories and therapies of Chinese medicine — reinforcing what is depleted, and clearing what is blocked or in excess.

Hypertension is the one of the highest risk factors in inducing stroke. 93% of hemorrhagic stroke patients have a history of hypertension, while 86% of ischemic stroke patients have a history of hypertension. A study into the effects of different types of qi gong on blood pressure was carried out in Shanghai Institute of Hypertension. The results showed that the decrease in blood pressure was related to the type of qi gong, the practice quality, and practice time. The effects were remarkable in those who practiced consistently and regularly, and long-term. Standing qi gong had a better effect in lowering blood pressure, compared with laying down (decub) qi gong; relaxing calming(sōng jìng) gong, had a better effect compared with imagination (yì shǒu) and inner force (nèi yǎng gōng); focusing in the lower dān tián had a better effect of lowering blood pressure, than focusing in the upper dān tián. Focus of down dān tián had a better depression effect compared with up dān tián.

fibrinogen and the effect of anti-thrombosis. These changes can reduce blood viscosity, and improve the quality of the blood. Even walking as exercise, if regular and long-term, can significantly decrease the blood viscosity, compared to not walking. A decrease in blood viscosity has the following benefits: improves circulation, reduces any blockages in the blood flow, and decreases blood pressure especially diastolic pressure. Therefore, aerobic exercise is beneficial in decreasing blood viscosity, improving blood flow, and reducing blood pressure to prevent stoke.

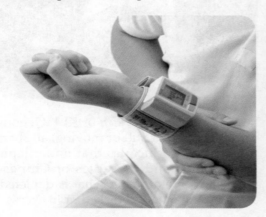

Persistence in a regular and suitable activity, especially aerobic endurance exercise, can increase plasma volume, and promote the dissolving effect of plasma

Case

Mr Zhang, an engineer, had a stroke because of over exertion before his retirement. He was treated in hospital for a month, and although his condition improved, he still had difficulty in walking, especially go up or downstairs, and in going to the bathroom. 20 days after being discharged, he participated in a qi gong workshop. To his surprise the effects of practicing qi gong was miraculous, and several of his symptoms were cured. His participation began when walking still remained challenging. His legs felt so heavy that they trembled, and his left arm and hand were numb. Throughout the hot summer he persisted in practicing, consequently becoming drenched in sweat. At the end of the one year workshop, his walking improved, and feeling returned to the hands. From his fourth month of practice he felt the qi coming out of his hands. When he was walking, he felt the qi entering his hands during his inhalation, and exiting his hands on his exhalation. As he became more flexible, the neurodermitis of his coccyx and arthritis in his knee were alleviated.

(2) Tai Ji Quan

Tai ji quan can be used for rehabilitation therapy; it originated from China, and is very popular among the masses there. It is a very common and efficient way to exercise and maintain health. Rehabilitation therapy is very beneficial for stroke patients; basic body exercises such as tai ji quan, and qi gong, are very popular and conducive to promoting rehabilitation outside the hospital.

There is scientific proof that tai ji quan should be prescribed as a physical exercise, because of the following effects: it prevents hypertension; improves the function of the cardiovascular system, respiratory system, and microcirculation in the body; enhances the movement and flexibility of the bones, muscles and joints; and promotes metabolism, digestion and absorption within the body.

Case

Ms. Chen suddenly had a stroke, aged 54, in 1995. Luckily, she was saved due to effective hospital care; however her speech remained unclear, and her walk unsteady, even after her discharge from hospital. Due to the paralysis she had to rely on her family, and she became very depressed. One day, while walking in the park, accompanied by her family, she saw tai ji quan being practiced. An elderly gentleman told her that tai ji can help during recovery of stroke. With the hope of regaining her mobility and independence, she was determined to practice tai ji. Af-ter 4 months of practicing, the flexibility in her hands and legs improved, and her speech became clearer than ever before. One day when her tai ji teacher saw sweat permeating her hands, she said with joy, " Congratulations, half of your body's blood is now moving smoothly". After a year of training, Ms. Chen looked like a healthy person. Ms Chen gained a big reward by practicing tai ji; besides the functional recovery of her limbs, she became open minded, and more patient and tolerable in all aspects of her life. Before the stroke she was very irritable, and easily lost her tem-

per. It can be very dangerous for someone with hypertension to lose their temper. Since practicing tai ji, she never lost her temper casually again.

Stroke patients who practice tai ji may improve their balance, reducing the risk of falls. The research to substantiate the results shown in the previous case study, is published in the Journal of Neurorehabilitation and Neural Repair, the lead author being Stephanie S. Y. Au-Yeung of Hong Kong Polytechnic University. The researchers recruited 136 volunteers who had had a stroke six months or longer ago. They were divided into two groups: one group did general exercises, and the other practiced a modified version of tai ji. The tai ji group was asked to attend a class once a week, and then practice at home for about three hours a week. After 12 weeks, both groups were tested on shifting their weight, reaching, and their ability to remain balanced whilst on a platform which moved like a bus. While the exercise group showed little improvement in balance, the tai ji group had made significant gains. The researchers indicated that the benefits of practicing tai ji were that the patients can practice by themselves once the exercise model was mastered. The report indicated that if the patients persisted in practicing tai ji in community centers, their balance would continue to improve.

Before the research, another report carried out by one of the cooperators Christina W. Y. Hui-Chan, already proved that the balance of healthy, elderly people can be improved by tai ji. Nevertheless, the researchers hoped that the improvement of balance, in stroke patients practicing tai ji, would be confirmed with this article.

(3) *Bā duàn jǐn*

Bā duàn jǐn is an independent, and complete body building system, originating from the Northern *Song* Dynasty, with a history of more than 800 years. It is very effective, traditional health exercises. *Bā duàn jǐn* has the following advantages: no exercise equipment or vast space is necessary; the movements are easy to learn; mistakes are difficult to make; and the effects are remarkable and definite. It is one of the treasures of Chinese culture, and is deeply loved by the people. *Bā duàn jǐn* is composed of eight movements; *bā* refers to eight, and *jǐn* refers to the exquisite luxury of silk, which reflects the gentle, coherent and fluid movements of the whole form.

Bā duàn jǐn is closely combined with the traditional Chinese health preservation and therapeutic concept. By practicing it, both the inside, spirit, and the outside, bone and skin, remain healthy. The whole set of movements are gentle and slow, smooth and coherent; motion balanced with stillness, relaxation balanced with concentration. It is very suitable for the elderly, those with poor health, as well as those in physical rehabilitation. It has the functions of softening the tendons, strengthening the bones, culti-

vating the qi to strengthen the body, promoting the qi to increase the circulation of blood, and coordinating the functions of internal organs. Modern research has confirmed that this set of exercises can improve neurological humoral regulation function, and promote blood circulation. It also has the effect of gently massaging the abdominal viscera. *Bā duàn jǐn* is beneficial for the nervous, cardiovascular, digestive, respiratory, and locomotory systems.

Bā duàn jǐn is composed of some simple movements, which have developed from therapeutic and diagnostic actions. Therefore, each action has a specific effect. You can focus on only one movement, several movements, or the whole sequence. Each movement and its effects are explained below.

Step 1 - Smooth triple energizer with two hands elevating to the sky

Both hands cross in front of the navel, before lifting to the sky, pulling and stretching back, and lifting and opening the chest and belly. Practicing this action increases the qi and fluid circulation, thereby nourishing the whole body.

Step 2 - Draw the bow on the left and right, as if shooting an eagle

Extend the shoulders and expand the chest, drawing a bow on the left and right, as if shooting an eagle. This movement is beautiful, and practicing it balances the qi in the chest and liver, eliminates dyspnea, cures rib ache, and also releases tightness in the back and shoulders. For those who sit working at a desk for long periods, and are under a great deal of stress, practicing this movement will increase lung capacity, increase the intake of oxygen, strengthen the will, and keep the body energized.

Step 3 - Lift one hand to regulate the spleen and stomach

The upward and downward movement of the left and right upper limbs stretches the belly, and massages the abdominal organs. This action can help the organs regulate qi movement, benefit digestion and absorption, and strengthen nutrition.

Step 4 - Look backward to cure strain and injuries

Five kinds of strain, and seven kinds of injury are common occurrences nowadays. Long-term exertion, with inadequate rest, induces the accumulation of injuries. Turn the head and twist the arms, to regulate the cervical vertebrae, which is the main pathway connecting the brain and organs (known as "*tian zhu*" in Chinese medicine). Thrusting the chest forward stimulates the thymus, which improves the brain activity, strengthens immunity and physical fitness, and maintains health.

Step 5 - Eliminate heart fire by shaking the head and buttocks

Bend the upper body forwards, and shake the buttocks; this is effective in treating distress, ulcers, halitosis, insomnia and dream disturbed sleep, burning urine, and constipation.

Step 6 - Strengthen the kidneys and waist with two hands catching the feet

Bend the body, extending backwards, and massage the back of the waist and legs. This action stimulates the *du mai* and the foot *taiyang* bladder channel, which is beneficial for the reproductive and urinary systems, as well as the back and waist muscles.

Step 7 - Strengthen the power by making a fist and glaring

Stand in horse riding stance, fists extended, staring forwards, to stimulate the foot *jueyin* liver channel, and to replenish the liver blood, smooth the flow of liver qi, and strengthen the bones and muscles. It is especially suitable for those with qi deficiency and blood stasis due to long-term sitting and bed rest.

Step 8 - Shake the back to cure disease

Stand on tiptoes, shaking the body, stretching the spine and massaging the organs. There is an old saying, "Shaking your body is much better for your health than walking a long distance". The action of shaking up and down on tiptoes causes the whole body to vibrate, is very comfortable, and can cure diseases. This is the final movement.

Traditional healthcare exercises such as qi gong, tai ji quan and *bā duàn jǐn* have a long history, deeply rooted in traditional Chinese culture. Practitioners have all been attracted by the simple movements, which have remarkable effects. It is believed that traditional healthcare exercises will become increasingly popular following the boom of body building.

3. Translated Research

To investigate the effects of long-term tai ji quan practice on the physical fitness of the elderly, Sha Kan-hui carried out a clinical trial. Method: 81 subjects, ranging in age from 60 to 75 years, were randomly assigned to a control group (38 people) or a treatment group (43 people). Patients with severe diseases, such as cardiovascular disease and diabetes, were excluded from this study. Agility, strength, balance, flexibility, hand grip, standing on one leg with eyes closed, and reaching forward in sitting position, were assessed in both groups. Results: Compared with the control group, the males in the treatment group displayed a quicker reaction time, an improvement in hand grip (P<0.01), an extended period of standing on one leg with eyes closed, and an improvement in the reaching distance when sitting (P<0.05). Compared with the control group, the females in the treatment group displayed a quicker reaction time, an improvement in hand grip (P<0.01), an extended period of standing on one leg with eyes closed, and an improvement in the reaching distance when sitting (P<0.05). Conclusion: Long-term tai ji quan practice is an effective way to improve the physical fitness of the elderly, and has a positive effect on slowing down the body's aging processes[25].

Li Xing-hai observed the effects of Ba Duan Jin qi gong on endothelium-dependent vasodilation in type 2 diabetes. Method: 79 type 2 diabetic subjects were randomly divided into a control group, and a qi gong exercise group. The exercise group began Ba Duan Jin qi gong classes for 6 months. The index of endothelium-dependent arterial dilation, the blood sugars and the blood fats of the control and exercise groups were measured separately, before exercises and the following day on an empty stomach, for a period of 6 months. Results: Ba Duan Jin exercises improves the index of endothelium-dependent arterial dilation, blood sugars and blood fats of type 2 diabetic patients, showing significant differences compared with the control group (P<0.05 and P<0.01). Conclusion: Ba Duan Jin qi gong is helpful to improve the function of endothelium-dependent arterial dilation and is successful in diabetic recovery[26].

Mao Yan explored the physiological mechanisms of different health benefits of tai ji quan and regular physical exercise, for senile women, by measuring blood lipid contents. Method: 120 senile women from Xi'an Municipal Senile University, aged between 55 to 72, were selected and randomly divided into a tai ji quan group, a regular physical exercise group, and a control group, with 40 women in each group. Questionnaire investigations and laboratory examinations were conducted. Results: After 48 weeks, the low-density lipoprotein cholesterol content of the senile women in the control group was 92. 24 ± 9. 68 mg/dl, in the tai ji quan group was 71. 09 ± 8. 03 mg/dl, and in the regular physical exercise group was 73. 64 ± 7. 29 mg/dL, displaying a significant difference between the tai ji quan group, comprehensive group, and the control group (P<0. 01). The serum triglyceride content of the senile women in the control group was 145. 28 ± 33. 86 mg/dl, in tai ji quan group was 128. 91 ± 37. 73 mg/dl, in the regular physical exercise group was 131. 10 ± 22. 63 mg/dL, again displaying a significant difference between the tai ji quan group, regular physical exercise group, and the control group (P<0. 01). Conclusion: Tai ji quan and regular physical exercise are both suitable, safe and effective methods for increasing health in senile people. To gain the most benefits, it is necessary for the senile women to carry out some form of exercise as well as practicing tai ji quan. Both tai ji quan and regular physical exercise have their own unique health characteristics[27].

Wang Fang studied the effects that different qi gong practices had on the quality of sleep in patients with type 2 diabetes, accompanied with insomnia. Method: 90 patients with type 2 diabetes, accompanied with insomnia, were randomly divided into a *Ba duan jin* qi gong group (group 1), Liu Zi-jue qi gong group (group 2), and a control group (group 3), with 30 in each group. Group 1 practiced Ba Duan Jin qi gong and Relaxation qi gong, group 2 practiced Liu Zi-jue qi gong and Relaxation qi gong, and the control group did not participate in any health preserving qi gong. The Pittsburgh Sleep Quality Index (PSQI) was used to measure the sleep quality, actual time taken to fall asleep, and actual sleep time. These were recorded for all patients before every qi

gong practice, and then 2 months and 4 months after treatment respectively. The data obtained was analyzed statistically by SPSS statistical software. Results: 78 patients were involved in the analysis, and the expulsion rate was 13.3%. After 4 months the comparison among groups showed that the total score of PSQI, the sleep quality and quantity, was significantly higher in group 1, than those in group 3 (P<0.05). The comparison in difference among groups showed that the sleep quality was higher in group 1 and 2, than that in group 3 (P<0. 05), while the total score of PSQI and sleep quantity was higher in group 1 than those in group 3 (P<0.05). The comparison within a group showed that the total score of PSQI and five other factors, except the factor of sleep time, were significantly increased in group 1 (P<0.05). The total score of PSQI and four other factors, except the factor of sleep time and insomnia, was significantly increased in group 2 (P<0.05). The actual time to fall asleep, and actual sleep time were significantly improved in group 1 and 2 (P<0.05). Conclusion: The health preserving qi gong of TCM can improve the sleep quality in patients with type 2 diabetes, accompanied by insomnia. Ba Duan Jin qi gong varies from Liu Zi Jue qi gong in their practice methods, and their effects also differ, when combined with Relaxation qi gong[28].

Wang Ze-ying investigated the effects of implementing small amounts of exercise into the lives of 100 stroke patients with qi deficiency. Method: 100 stroke patients with qi deficiency were randomly divided into 2 groups, the experimental group and the control group. Control group: Walking fast, or some other active exercise, for at least 30 minutes, 2 -3 times per day, to increase activity as much as possible. Control group: Doing active exercises but not weight training, as much as possible, for 5- 10 minutes, 2 -3 times per day. Results: There were statistical differences in the scale of qi deficiency, measured on the National Institutes of Health Stroke Scale (NIHSS) and Barthel Index (BI) between the two groups (P<0.05), complications and rehospitalization occurred less in the experimental group (P<0.05), and the medical satisfaction was higher than the control group (P<0.05). Conclusion: Compared with the health education of modern medicine, the stroke patients with qi deficiency whose health education included a small amount of exercise, showed improvements in their daily activities, and a decrease in any complications or rehospitalization visits[29].

In order to compare effects of different exercise intensities on cardiovascular functions in the elderly, Ran Bin carried out a clinical trial. Method: 120 cases of retired elderly people were randomly divided into 3 groups: walking group, tai ji quan group and aerobics group. They participated in the activities for three months, and cardiovascular functions were compared before and after exercise.

Results: after three months of exercise, the heart rates in all three groups were lower than that before the exercise program, but there was no significant difference between the three groups (P>0.05) Blood pressure had significantly decreased after the 3 months, particularly in the tai ji quan group and aerobics group. C0, SV, SI, CI and PEP all significantly increased after exercise, with particularly significant differences in the tai ji quan group and aerobics group (P<0.05). Conclusion: By adopting a standard aerobic exercise program the cardiovascular function can improve, disease can be prevented, and the aging process can be delayed in the elderly, resulting in good health, fitness and longevity[30].

Liu Shan-yun selected the middle aged and the elderly to research the effects of tai ji quan on blood lipids and the immune function. Results: After 16 weeks of tai ji quan practice the blood lipids and lipoprotein metabolism improved, and increased the level of Immunoglobulin. Conclusion: This result indicated that moderate exercise can prevent abnormal blood lipids, decreasing the risk of heart and blood disease[31].

Li Chuan-wu studied the effect of tai ji quan on the endothelial diastolic function in 32 elderly men. Results: (1) After exercise, the triglyeride, total cholesterol and low-density lipoprotein cholesterol all decreased significantly (P<0.05), whilst the high-density lipoprotein cholesterol and plasma NO increased significantly (P<0.05, 0.01). There was no obvious change in the control group's levels before and after exercise. (2) The inner diameter of the humerus artery in the exercise group showed no marked changes, but the reactive diastolic degree showed a significant increase (P<0.05). The control group showed no changes. Conclusion: Tai ji quan exercise may improve endothelial diastolic function in the elderly, due to the decreased levels of blood fat and the increase in plasma NO[32].

Li Zhao-wei observed the curative effect of five-animal exercises in patients with dyslipidemia. Methods: 66 patients with dyslipidemia were divided randomly into two groups, with 33 cases in the treatment group treated by five-animal exercises, and 33 cases in the control group treated by jogging. Patients of both groups received dietary therapy also. After two courses of treatments (16 weeks), they tested TC, TG, LDL-C, HDL-C and the compliance rate in both groups. Results: After treatment TC, TG and LDL-C levels of the treatment group decreased significantly (P<0.01), while the HDL-C of this group increased significantly (P<0.05). TC, TG and LDL-C levels in the treatment group changed much more dramatically, than those of the control group (P<0.05). In addition, the compliance rate in the treatment group was higher than that in the control group (P<0.05). Conclusion: Five-animal exercises are effective for patients with dyslipidemia[33].

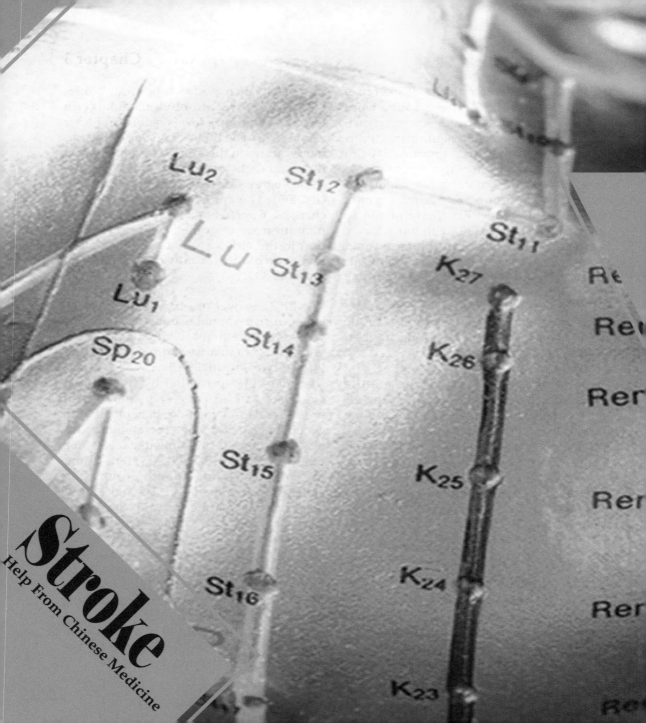

Chapter 4

How Does Chinese Medicine Help Manage Stroke?

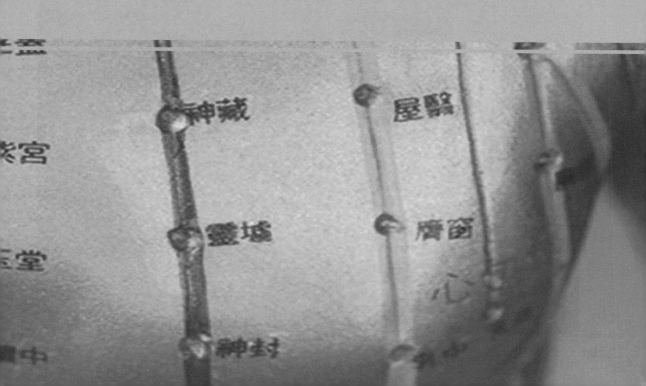

In stroke prevention, treatment and rehabilitation, TCM has many other therapies to offer besides diet therapy and exercises. These include acupuncture, cupping, massage, *guā shā*, medicated baths, and fumigation, which are all very special and unique ways to help recovery after stroke.

Acupuncture and Moxibustion

1. What Is Acupuncture and Moxibustion?

(1) Zhēn jiŭ 灸

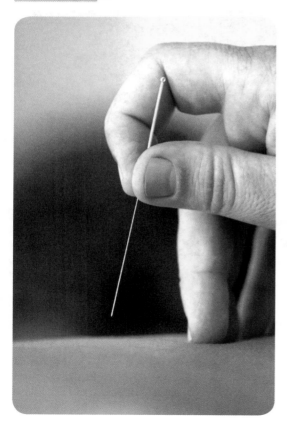

Zhēn jiŭ is a Chinese term that refers to acupuncture and moxibustion, the treatment methods that have been characteristic of Chinese medicine for thousands of years. Acupuncture treatment involves special needling instruments that are used to prick points on the channels and collaterals, in order to influence the functions and structures of the body, to treat and prevent disease. Acupuncture and moxibustion is a medicine, invented and developed by the Chinese, during a long history of fighting against disease, as well as the crystallization of experiences of the Chinese doctors in their medical practices. As early as the remote Stone Age, people began to use small pieces of sharp stone (called "*biǎn* stones", the predecessor of filiform needles), to stimulate the diseased area of the body to treat diseases. With the development of social communities, people began to use metals to make copper, iron, gold and silver needles, rather than use the stone needles. Moxibustion therapy was devised after the invention of fire; people gradually discovered that a comfortable sensation might be felt, or an illness or pain relieved when the body was warmed or blistered by fire, with repeated use. Plants, such as mugwort, ignited easily, and had the ability to warm and dredge channels and collaterals. It was selected as the substance for moxibution, and hence the development of the practice of moxibustion started.

The first record of acupuncture is found in the *The Yellow Emperor's Internal Classic,* compiled over 2,000 years ago. It is an important component of Chinese medicine. For thousands of years, acupuncture and moxibustion have not only exerted a great influence on the Chinese medical care, but this distribution of knowledge has also spread to foreign countries, and contributed to the medical care in these countries too. In the 6th century, acupuncture and moxibustion were introduced to other Eastern and Western countries; they were integrated into Korea in A.D.541, and introduced to Japan in A.D.562.

These days, acupuncture is everywhere. Searching online, one can read hundreds of reports of research involved in the scientific exploration of this ancient art. Acupuncture and moxibustion have been proven effective in various diseases from cardiology to psychology. One reason these techniques are so popular is that they are absolutely safe, when properly administered by a trained acupuncturist, although the thought of being needled can be unsettling to many first time patients. For most people in the West, it is difficult to understand how a fine needle inserted

into the foot can relieve a headache, why a fetus's position can be reversed by needling a toe, or how puncturing a spot on the wrist can treat insomnia. All of these actions are easily explained in the language of Chinese medicine, but there are still many theories on what exactly is at work in modern scientific terms. In order to understand acupuncture, moxibustion, and channel theory, an understanding of Chinese medical theory is necessary[34].

(2) *Jīng luò* ℒ

In the theory of Chinese medicine, the human body is an organic whole, and the internal organs, external surface, and extremities are connected to each other by a network called *jīng luò* (channels and collaterals). Channels refer to "go through" or "a path". The channels are

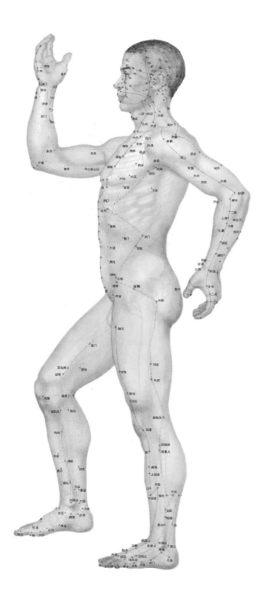

the main thoroughfares, thick and large, that connect the interior and exterior of the body with the internal organs. The collaterals are the branches of the channels, thin and small. They run transversely and superficially, and form a lattice network that connects every part of the body in an intricate web. Channels and collaterals are the pathways through which the qi and blood of the body circulates, so we can see they have a close relationship with the activities of human life.

(3) Formation of the theory of channels

◆ Obtained from pathological and anatomical knowledge

By the method of direct observation, ancient people gained a degree of knowledge about blood vessels, muscles and tendons, bones, and organs, as well as the interrelationships between them, thus providing a basis for the formation of the theory of channels.

◆ Deduction of the pathological phenomena over the body

In clinical practice, it has been found that certain visceral disorders may manifest on the corresponding superficial area of the body, where some pathological phenomena may occur. For example, tenderness, nodes, rashes, and changes in luster. Clinically: Tenderness can be found near EX-LE 7 (*lán wěi*, 阑尾) in a patient with appendicitis. When one organ becomes diseased, pressing the corresponding superficial area in the body may relieve the pain inside. Thereby, it is inferred that there are special routes associating these acupoints, which serves as another basis for the formation of the theory.

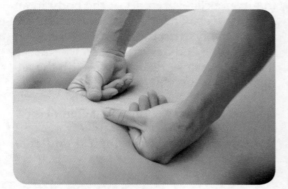

◆ Observation and deduction on induction and transmission phenomena of acupuncture and moxibustion

If the needles are accurately inserted into the right acupoints, the patient will experience a feeling of soreness, numbness, heaviness, distention, or tingling, which is also called needling sensation or *dé qì* (arrival of qi), and may also transmit along certain routes to distant areas. When performing the technique of health preservation in qi gong, practitioners who concentrate their mind on Dantian point (the central area below the umbilicus), usually have a sense of qi flowing along certain routes. This kind of sense and transmission is one important basis for the formation of the theory of channels.

◆ Summary of the therapeutic effects of acupoints

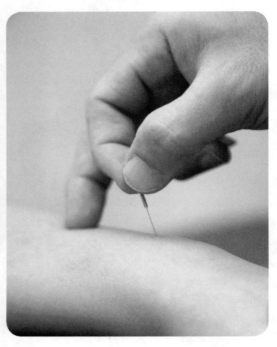

When trying to summarize and analyze the main therapeutic effects of acupoints, ancient people found that acupoints with similar functions usually followed the same route in a similar order. Clinical link: Acupoints which are distributed over the upper and lateral aspect of the chest, and the anterior border of the medial side of the upper arm, are responsible for treating disorders of the lung, trachea, and throat, as well as certain disorders on the surface of the body. So it is presumed that the acupoints are connected with each other through some particular pathways, which shows the great importance to the formation of the concept of channels.

(4)The channel system ♋

The channel-collateral system is composed of the twelve regular channels, the eight channels, the twelve divergent channels, the twelve muscles regions and the twelve cutaneous regions, the fifteen collaterals, and the minute and superficial collaterals. Amongst these, the twelve regular channels can be seen as the primary system. Running transversely and longitudinally, they intersect with each other, both in the interior and exterior of the body, forming a complete system.

The Channel System

Channel system	Channels	Twelve regular channels	Three yin channels of the hand	-Lung -Heart -Pericardium
			Three yang channels of the hand	-Large intestine -Small intestine -Triple burner
			Three yin channels of the foot	-Spleen -Kidney -Liver
			Three yang channels of the foot	-Stomach -Urinary bladder -Gallbladder
		Eight extraordinary vessels Twelve divergent channels		
	Collaterals	Fifteen network vessels Grandchild network vessels Superficial network vessel		
	Twelve sinew channels			
	Twelve cutaneous regions			

The channels transport qi and blood, connect the internal organs and the limbs, as well as the upper body to the lower body, the interior to the exterior, and regulate all parts of the body. Qi flows through the channels in a certain sequence. There are fourteen main channels running vertically up and down the surface of the body; twelve of the channels are symmetrical on the left and right sides of the body, and there are also two unpaired channels, which run up the mid-line of the abdomen to the head, and along the spine to the head. It reflects the regularity of some of the physiological and pathological phenomena that occur within the human body. It also has implications for guiding treatment in clinic.

(5) Acupoints

Acupoints are the specific sites through which the qi of the *zang-fu* organs and channels is transported to the body's surface, and through which acupuncture and moxibution, and other therapies, are applied by external stimulation. Distributed on their related channel pathways, acupoints are closely linked with the channels and collaterals. So the acupoints should not be regarded as superficial points alone, but as special sites which connect with each other, and through which the internal tissues and organs are related. The channels-collaterals connect the whole body, both interiorly and exteriorly, and diseases of the body can be treated by puncturing the points on the body surface to regulate the related channels, *zang-fu* organs, and the circulation of qi and blood.

The functions of acupuncture points are accessed by needling, through moxibustion, and via other manual techniques. By stimulating the acupoints, or the gates of this network, the body will be influenced, moving naturally towards healing. Acupoints are the openings of the channels and collaterals. Inserting needles into these points will stimulate, or block, the flow of qi and blood. When properly administered, the flow of qi and blood will be smoothed, and organ functions will be restored. Weakness is strengthened, while excess is reduced. Therefore balance is reestablished, and health is regained.

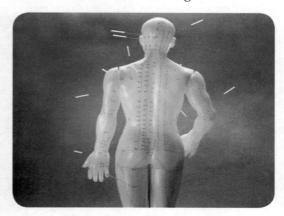

◆ **Different categories of acupuncture points**

Acupoints are classified into three categories: acupoints of the fourteen channels, extraordinary points and Ashi points.

◆ Points of the fourteen channels

These are the points that lie along the twelve regular channels, and the two channels that run up the mid-line of the body, *du mai* and *ren mai*. In total there are 361 acupoints. These points have numerous functions that relate to their location, channel, and corresponding organ. Since the points are distributed on the course of the fourteen channels, the points are very closely related to the channels. Not only can they treat diseases of the channels themselves, but also reflect disorders of the fourteen channels and the related *zang-fu* organs. Many belong to special categories that have specific uses. These points make up the majority of acupuncture points on the body. Specific points refer to those acupoints on the fourteen channels that have special properties. Since they have different therapeutic effects, the ancient doctors gave them different names. Knowing the meaning, indications and clinical applications of these points is of upmost importance clinically, for point selection. The commonly used specific points are the five shu points, the yuan points, the luo points, the back shu points, the front mu points, the eight confluence points, the intersection points, the eight influential points, the xi points, and the lower he points.

◆ Non-channel points

These points have fixed locations, but do not lie on any of the fourteen channels.

These points are especially effective in the treatment of certain diseases. They often have specific functions that are sometimes reflected in their names. For instance, *lán wěi xué*, which means appendix point in Chinese, treats appendicitis, and *tài yáng*, located at the temples, is used to treat headaches.

◆ *Ā shì* points

Ā shì points are non-channel points that do not have fixed names or locations. *Ā shi* is what a patient would say in Chinese when the doctor pushes on a painful point. It literally means "Ah, that's it." In pain syndromes *ā shì* points are searched for, and then needled, in order to eliminate stagnation in the area. They are tender spots and other reactive spots, which are used as sites for needling and moxibution. *Ā shì* points are usually near the affected area, but not necessarily.

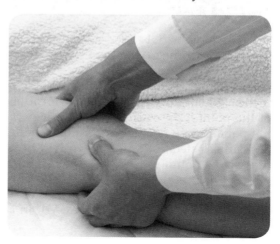

(6) Acupuncture

◆ Acupuncture needles

In ancient times there were nine types of needles, though only six of these are commonly used today. These needles vary in length, width of the shaft, and shape of the tip. In order to avoid being infected among patients, sterile needles that are inserted only once are commonly used now.

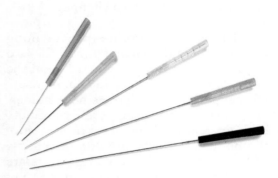

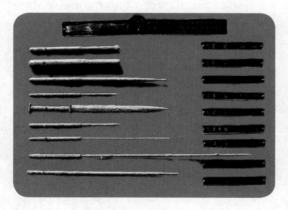

The most widely used needle in clinic is the filiform needle, currently made of stainless steel, and usually between 0.5-1.5 inches long (1.5-4.5 cm), but can be up to 5 inches (15 cm), depending on the location of the point to be needled, and the size of the patient. The needles are usually made of stainless steel, but gold and silver needles are sometimes used, and they should be kept and maintained with great care to avoid damage. The needles are used on one patient, and then disposed of in a medical sharps container.

◆ Acupuncture positions

Different positions are used, based on the points selected. As long as the patient feels comfortable, any position is suitable. Common positions are shown in the following pictures.

◆ Clean needling practice

Acupuncturists are required to take a course called the "Clean Needle Technique" to train them how to handle, insert, and remove needles so both patient and practitioner are protected from any kind of contamination. The acupuncturist will wash his or her hands thoroughly, with soap and water, before and after treatment, and the points to be needled will be disinfected by swabbing the point with a cotton swab dipped in 75% alcohol. Anything that punctures the skin will be sterile, and any other implements used in treatment will be thoroughly sanitized between patients.

2. How Can Acupuncture Help Stroke?

As one of the most commonly used treatments for sequelas of stroke, acupuncture with characteristics of great effectiveness, simplicity, affordability, safety, and non-toxic side effects, has been accepted by patients. Its mechanism is mainly manifested in the following aspects:

➢ In the acute phase of cerebral hemorrhage, the emphasis of the therapeutic effect of acupuncture is focused on restoring consciousness, and improving cortical function, so that the repressed function of cerebral cortex can be stimulated, which is conducive to treatment[35,36].

➢ For the period of stroke recovery and sequelae, the target of acupuncture is mainly focused on improving the brain tissue metabolic disorders, reducing free radicals injury to the cranial nerve generated by brain cell membrane and membrane lipid peroxides, and speeding up the removal of free radicals, to produce a protective effect. Modern studies have also shown that acupuncture can improve electromyographic activity of the limbs, thus improving lower limb motor functions[37]. Signals stimulated by acupuncture, pass up into the primary and senior nerve centers, to facilitate the resumption of interrupted contact between the central and peripheral nerve, resulting in compensatory functions, thus further promoting the functional recovery of paralyzed limbs[38,39].

It is definite that acupuncture can treat stroke, but when should acupuncture treatment begin? Studies have shown that in early stage stroke, patients treated with acupuncture in a timely manner, can improve the self repair of and compensatory capacity of the nervous system, accelerate the natural recovery process, shorten the course, lay a good foundation for functional recovery, reduce the incidence of deformity, and improve the quality of life, so that patients can live amongst their family and society[40,41]. Therefore, acupuncture can be carried out in the early stage, as long as the vital signs are stable, and the patient is conscious. Patients with stroke can receive acupuncture treatment 48 hours after the onset of illness, or after one week for patients with cerebral hemorrhage[42].

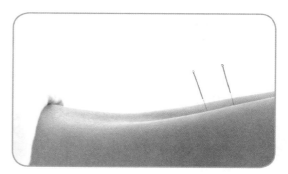

Case

Mr. Wang, a 55 years old male worker, made his first visit in December 1990.

History: the patient was sent to the hospital emergency room on June 12, 1990, with his right limb out of action, aphasia, and wandering. After 7 days, the patient's condition improved, and he was discharged for acupuncture treatment. Examination: Left side nasolabial sulcus became shallow, mouth deviated to the left side, clear consciousness, dribbling, unclear speech, complete paralysis in the right upper and lower limbs, muscular strength 0, the right limb obtuse sensation, tendon reflex and biceps reflex, triceps reflex augmentation, positive Babinski sign, blood pressure 22/14kPa. CT showing left basal ganglia infarction. Diagnosis: Stroke. Treatment: A treatment course (10 days) of acupuncture on the main points and distribution points of the lower limbs. After this course, the dribbling stopped, the right nasolabial sulcus returned to normal, facial paralysis recovered, coherent speech was restored to enable a simple dialogue, the right upper and lower limbs could be elevated, and walking with support was possible. Speech returned after 2 courses of treatment. The function returned to the right arm, although the muscle remained weak. The right leg became fully functional, although the ankle remained a little

weak. The patient could walk alone. Blood pressure was 18/11kPa. After another treatment, the blood pressure was stable, the pathologic reflex disappeared, and the sensory and limb functions were restored. He was able to live by himself and eventually returned to work. The follow up visit showed no relapse.

(1) Commonly used acupuncture points

There are hundreds of points on the human body, most of which are situated along the fourteen main channels. Some of the points are more commonly used than others. The points selected to help stroke can vary greatly, according to the patterns, the patient, and the practitioner's training and experience. The final prescription or point selection depends upon your specific condition, and the practitioner's judgment. The action of every point is to regulate yin and yang, the difference is in what exact way each point works. Some points work on the qi aspect, while others may work on the blood; some are warming, and others are cooling. Most point functions have not been verified by modern research, but for some of the more important points, some research has been done. Below are some photos and descriptions of commonly used points in the treatment of stroke. Of course all patients are different, so not everyone will get all of these points. But since some of these are major points, everyone is likely to experience at least a couple of these points during the course of treatment. Many of the points featured are on the spleen and stomach channels, since these organs are the main organs of digestion.

DU 20 (*bǎi huì*, 百会)

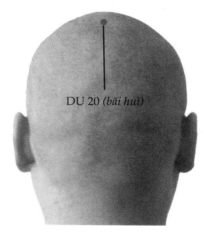

DU 20 (*bǎi huì*)

This point lies at the vertex, 5 *cun* directly above the median of the anterior hairline, or the midpoint of the line joining two auricular apexes. To locate simply, it is the crossing point of the anterior midline channels, and the line connecting both ear apexes. DU 20 is a very important point, and used frequently for many disorders. Its name means "100 channels intersection" and is a crossing point for the *du mai*, and foot *taiyang* channels in

Chinese medicine. Its location at an important intersection helps it to regulate qi and blood, and it is harmonizing in many ways. It is used to treat headaches, vertigo, aphasia from apoplexy, epilepsy and mania, prolapse of the uterus, insomnia and many emotional disorders. Wind easily attacks the upper part and surface of body, therefore DU 20 is selected to dispel wind from the upper part, and to regulate the qi movement of the *du mai*, and induce resuscitation to regain consciousness. Needling method: Puncturing subcutaneously 0.5-0.8 *cun*. Functions: Improves health, prolongs life, stimulates and increases the body's yang qi, and regulates the vascular system of the heart and brain. DU 20 is closely connected with the brain, and regulates brain functions to prevent strokes. It is the intersection of many channels, and so travels all over the body. The head is the convergence of yang qi, the origin of all channels, and DU 20 is the convergence of all *jīng* qi. It is a yang point, but also connects to the yin, so plays an important role for regulating the body's yin and yang balance.

ST 36 (*zú sān lǐ*, 足三里)

Arguably the most important point on the body, ST 36, which means "leg three mile", is the primary point used when the body's qi is weak. The name informs the practitioner that needling here will help the patient walk three more miles on their life journey. Another interpretation of the name describes how by needling this point, qi and blood are filled to such an amount that it covers three square miles. It is located on the stomach channel, and can be used for any digestive disorder as well. Since the body's qi is largely produced by the digestive system, the importance of good digestion to health cannot be exaggerated. This is especially true in people with weight difficulties, where needling this point can improve the function of both the spleen and stomach, allowing for more efficient absorption and elimination. ST 36 is located roughly one hand's breadth (4 fingers) from the bottom of the knee cap, on the outside of the leg. It is often somewhat sensitive when pressed. ST 36 may lower blood pressure, invigorate the spleen and eliminate dampness, and remove phlegm to prevent stroke.

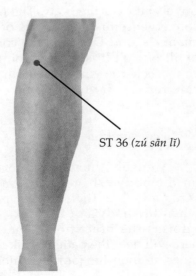

ST 36 (*zú sān lǐ*)

SP 6 (*sān yīn jiāo*, 三阴交)

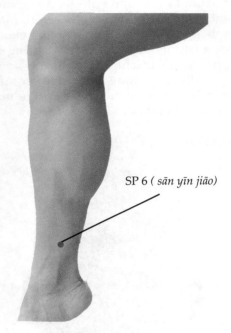

SP 6 (*sān yīn jiāo*)

SP 6 is located on the inner leg, roughly one hand's breadth (4 fingers) above the tip of the medial malleolus, in the muscle behind the shin bone. This point lies on a yin portion of the body, the inner lower leg. It is a very important point, and often used for many disorders. Its name means "three yin intersection", and it is a crossing point for the spleen, liver, and kidney channels, all of which are considered yin channels in Chinese medicine. Its location at an important intersection helps it to regulate the organ functions of the spleen, liver, and kidney in many ways. It is frequently used for digestive disorders, and is also often employed in treating gynecological problems, and many emotional disorders. Research has shown this point is able to increase urinary output in order to eliminate excess water, and adjust water metabolism. Needling method: Puncturing 1-1.5 cun vertically.

SP 9 (*yīn líng quán*, 阴陵泉)

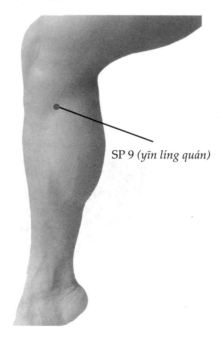

SP 9 (*yīn líng quán*)

this characteristic is reflected in the name. Its function is to regulate the ability of the spleen to transform water. It is stagnant water that forms phlegm, which is one of the significant causes of stroke. Because of this, it is essential in the treatment of stroke.

ST 40 (*fēng lóng*, 丰隆)

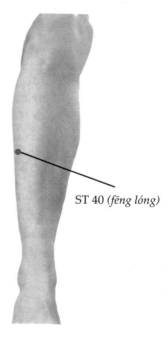

ST 40 (*fēng lóng*)

SP 9 is located just under the inside of the knee, on the front of the calf muscle, behind the bone. It is the uniting point of the spleen channel. The name means "spring from the mound". As the uniting point, this is the place where fluid and essence from the spleen channel gather, and

ST 40 is located on the outer lower leg, half the distance between the knee cap and the outer ankle bone, and two knuckles back from the shin. It is the stomach channel, and is the network point of the spleen channel. This is the point on the channel where the flow of qi has a connection to the stomach's paired organ, the spleen. This point is often used in problems with phlegm or dampness. Its name means "plentiful mound" which tells us that ST 40 can treat any problem where there is too much of a substance accumulated in the spleen or stomach channels. Research has shown this point to be effective in freeing the bowels, and reducing the levels of fat in the blood. ST 40 is the *luo* point of the stomach channel, which means being connected with the spleen channel. It may lower blood pressure, invigorate the spleen and eliminate dampness, and remove phlegm to prevent stroke.

RN 4 (*guān yuán*, 关元)

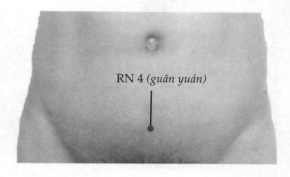

RN 4 (*guān yuán*)

RN 4 is located roughly one hand's breadth (4 fingers) below the belly button on the mid-line of the abdomen. Located on a very yin portion of the body, the lower abdomen, RN 4 helps to nourish the yin of the liver and kidneys, as well as strengthening qi. The point lies on the *ren mai*, and is also known as "The Sea of Yin". It is a key point for strengthening the body, and is a commonly used point for weak patients, and those with problems in the lower abdomen and pelvic region. It is used to regulate disorders of the reproductive system: emissions, impotence, irregular menstruation, disorders of the urinary system, and disorders of the digestive system. It also has a tonifying effect. Needling method: puncturing 1-2 *cun*.

GB 20 (*fēng chí*, 风池)

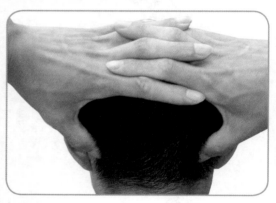

GB 20 is located in the depression between the upper portion of the sterno-cleidomastoid muscle and the trapezius. It is an intersection point of the foot *shaoyang* channels and *yangwei* vessel. This point is often used for headaches, pain and stiffness of the neck, blurred vision, red and painful eyes, rhinorrhea, tinnitus, common cold, fever, malaria, wind stroke, epilepsy, febrile diseases, and goiter.

Needling method: pricking 0.8-1.2 cun obliquely towards the tip of the nose, or towards DU 16 (*fēng fǔ*) horizontally. Deep puncturing is prohibited.

DU 16 (*fēng fǔ*, 风府)

DU 16 lies 1 *cun* directly above the median of the posterior hairline, and directly below the occipital protuberance, in the depression between the two sides of the trapezius muscle. DU 16 is a very important point, and often used for many disorders. It is an intersection point of the *du mai* and foot *taiyang* channels. Its location helps it to regulate the brain function in many ways. It is often employed in treating headaches, stiffness of the neck, vertigo, epilepsy, and mania.

Needling method: pricking perpendicularly or obliquely 0.5-1 *cun*. Deep puncturing is prohibited.

GB 20 belongs to the foot *shaoyang* channel, while DU 16 belongs to the *du mai*, both of which lie on the neck. From the anatomical analysis, the two acupoints are situated on the surface of the big hole of occipital bone and bulbar center, through which the points improve the function of brain tissue. GB 20 and DU 16 are the main points in the treatment of stroke with acupuncture. In the process of manipulation, the correct angle and depth are important for improving therapeutic effect.

(2) Moxibustion

Moxibustion is a therapy in which burning moxa is used to produce a heat stimulation to the body. It affects the function of the channels and points, to prevent and treat disease. Moxibustion is not for everyone. It is indicated mainly for patients suffering from cold or stagnation. It is not used on anyone diagnosed with too much heat. For patients with deficient syndromes, particularly those involving deficient spleen or kidney yang, moxibustion is often used. For people who have asthma or other respiratory problems, smokeless moxa can be used.

◆ **Direct moxibustion**

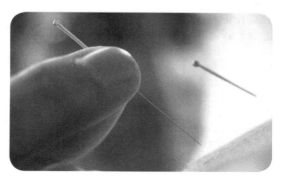

Direct moxibustion is commonly used. Place an appropriately sized moxa cone directly on the point and ignite it. This method can be classified into scarring moxibustion, and non-scarring moxibustion. Scarring moxibustion is also called festering moxibustion: prior to moxibustion, apply a small amount of garlic to the area around the point, in order to increase the adhesion and stimulation of the moxa cone to the skin. An appropriately sized moxa cone is placed on the point and ignited. Each cone should be completely burnt out and the ash removed, before repeating. Repeat this procedure for the required number of moxa cones. Patting the skin gently with the hand, around the point, can be used to alleviate pain if is very strong. In a normal situation, one week after the moxibustion the local area festers and a post-moxibustion sore will form. After 5-6 weeks, the post-moxibustion sore will heal by itself, and the scab falls off, leaving a small scar. Scarring moxibustion may not be used unless the patient agrees to cooperate before the treatment begins. Non-scarring moxibustion: apply a small amount of vaseline to the area around the point, in order to increase the adhesion of the moxa cone to the skin. An appropriately sized moxa cone is placed directly on the point and ignited. When the patient begins to feel a burning sensation, remove the cone, replacing it with another one on the same area. Because the skin is not burnt there is no scar formation after the treatment.

◆ Indirect moxibustion

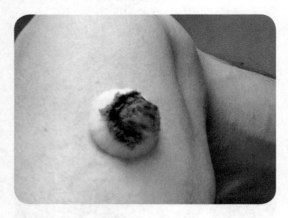

Indirect moxibustion is another method; the ignited moxa is insulated from the skin, by a cake of medicinal substance. Fresh ginger, garlic, salt, and monkshood (aconite) are often used. With a moxa stick, a practitioner holds the stick roughly 1.5 inches (4.5 cm) above the skin, keeping it in place until the skin becomes red or appears congested. When garlic, ginger, or salt is used with moxibustion, they provide a buffer from the heat of the moxa, as well as adding their own properties to the therapeutic effect. These forms of treatment do not usually cause pain or leave any blistering or scars, although the skin may remain red for a while. It usually causes a very pleasant sensation that patients enjoy.

Practitioners also sometimes place the moxa cone on top of an acupuncture needle and burn it. If good ventilation is not available, heat can also be applied to points from an electrical source designed for this purpose as well.

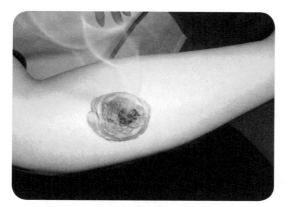

blood vessels. Moxibustion is not applied on the abdomen, or lumbosacral region in pregnant women.

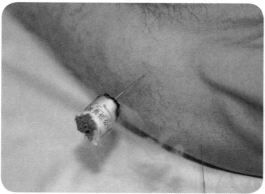

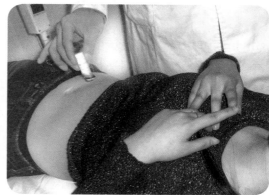

◆ Attention

During treatment, attention should be paid to prevent burning the clothes or skin. Moxibustion is not applicable for excessive heat syndrome and fever due to yin deficiency. Scarring moxibustion is not applied on the face, the five sensory organs, and areas in the vicinity of the large

(3) Other techniques

Although acupuncture and moxibustion are the main techniques used by practitioners of Chinese medicine, there are a variety of other techniques that may be used. These include but are not limited to cupping, *guā shā*, and plum-blossom needling.

◆ Scalp acupuncture

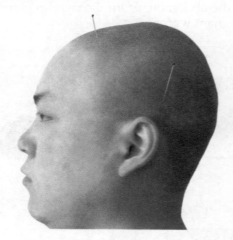

Scalp acupuncture is a therapy in which acupuncture and/or moxibustion are used to stimulate the points, as well as channels and collaterals on the head, to regulate the movement of qi and blood, and the functions of *zang-fu* organs. Some choose related points on the head to treat diseases according to the theory of *zang-fu* organs and the theory of the channels and collaterals, while others needle the corresponding stimulating areas on the scalp, according to the action location of the cerebral cortex[43]. Its theoretical foundation includes the theory of channels and collaterals, the theory of the action location of cerebral cortex, and the theory of holographic biology. Doctors used it alone, or in combination with body acupuncture and moxibustion, not only for the central nerve diseases, but also for other various diseases and symptoms, as well as cortex-

internal organ dysfunctions, with satisfactory therapeutic effects[44].

Treatment method using scalp acupuncture for stroke: select mainly the *dǐng niè qián xié xiàn* (MS 6), *dǐng niè hòu xié xiàn* (MS 7) on the opposite side, *é páng xiàn* II (MS 3). *Niè qián xiàn* (MS 10) is used for improving slurred speech. Needling method: use 1.5-2 *cun* mini needles. Puncture horizontally for 3-5 cm. Twist them constantly at the speed of 200 times per minute, for about 2-3 minutes. Give a treatment everyday, or once every other day. 10 treatments make a course. When one course is finished wait 3-5 days, then continue with a second course.

◆ Auricular acupuncture (ear acupuncture)

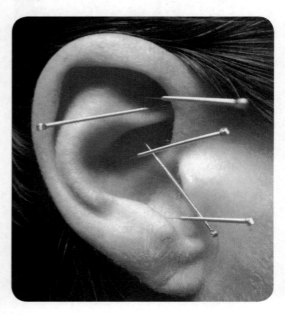

Auricular therapy treats and prevents diseases by stimulating certain points on the auricle of the ear, with needles or other methods. Auricular therapy has a long history in China.

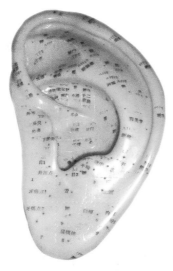

Similar to reflexology, the ear represents a microsystem of the entire body. The shape of the ear is like looking at a curled up fetus upside down, with the head as the lobe and the legs curled up to form the top of the ear. The entire human body with all its different parts and organs has been mapped out. Treatment is usually performed by probing the ear for sensitive points, and then needling these points. For instance, if a patient has a stomach problem, the practitioner will probe for the most sensitive point in the vicinity of the stomach point, and then choose that point to needle[45].

A popular technique is to place a small seed, metal pellet, or tiny needle on an ear point and keep it in place with a small piece of tape. These objects will then provide a constant stimulation to the points chosen. Usually you will be instructed to press, or rub each of these points several times a day for a few minutes. This convenient form of therapy allows for around the clock treatment. Normally the tape can be taken off in three or four days. Auricular therapy using seeds, pellets, or magnets is very popular because there is no need to use needles. It is safe, reliable, easy to perform, and has long standing therapeutic effects without side effects.

Method: press gently, slowly, and evenly on the disease related corresponding area with a probe, stick, match or the handle of a filiform needle, to look for tender spots. Auricular points should be swabbed with 2% iodine tincture, and 75% alcohol as a routine precaution. You can stick a magnetic sphere, vaccaria seed, or radish seed with a piece of adhesive plaster. Ask the patient to press the points 2-4 times a day, by themselves. Change the points after 3-5 days[46].

◆ Cupping

Cupping is a therapy in which a jar (glass cup, bamboo jar, pottery jar) is attached to an area of the skin's surface, to cause warm stimulation, and local congestion. This is achieved by removing the

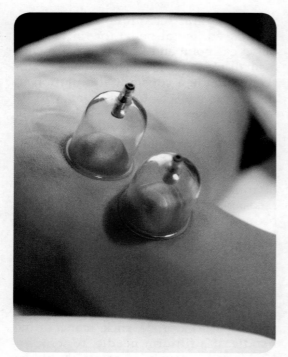

methods, rapid cupping methods, cupping with bloodletting, and acupuncture cupping methods. Select the most suitable size cup, according to the size of the selected area. It is not suitable to apply cupping to a patient with skin ulcers, edema, an allergic skin reaction, or on an area overlying large blood vessels. It is also not advisable to apply cupping on the abdominal and lumbosacral region of pregnant women. It is not advisable to apply cupping on a patient with spontaneous hemorrhage that is difficult to stop when injured. Before applying cupping on the face or any area which is exposed, permission must be given by the patient. Retention of the cup may produce bruising.

◆ *Gua sha*

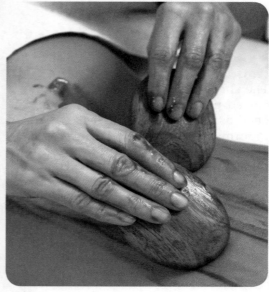

air in a jar, created by introducing heat in the form of an ignited material. The most commonly used cupping method is "fire twinkling" method. Ignite a piece of paper or a cotton ball soaked with 95% alcohol, and hold with forceps. Put it into the cup, and circle it around inside 1-3 times. Remove it, placing the cup on the selected position. Retain the cup in the position for about 10-15 minutes. Remove the cup after it begins to draw the blood stasis to the surface. Hold the cup with the left hand, pressing the skin around the rim of the cup with the right hand to let air in. The cup is easily removed. There are moving cupping

Guā shā (skin scraping), as one of the traditional natural therapies, is based on the theory of twelve skin regions in TCM, with tools (such as horns, jade, cups) scraping relevant parts of the skin, to promote blood circulation for removing blood stasis and to regulate the flow of qi to remove stagnation. It is used in many cultures, and usually used for pain that is caused by an invasion of pathogenic wind, cold or heat, and is still quite superficial in the body. The rapid, light scraping techniques are not painful, but will elicit slight bruising in the area. These bruises are very superficial, are not painful, and are a sign that the congestion causing pain has been activated and is leaving the body. The purpose of skin scrapping is to cause redness and congestion at the local painful area, so that channel points congest, local micro-circulation improves, pathogens are eliminated, vital qi is strengthened, qi and blood is harmonized, wind pathogens are dispelled, heat is cleared and blood is cooled, blood circulation is promoted to remove obstructions in the collaterals, channels are warmed to dispel cold, pathogenic wind is dispelled from the muscles, toxicity is removed from swellings, and the body's own resistance and immunity is enhanced.

(4) Cautions and contraindications

Acupuncture and its adjunct modalities are safe therapies. However, there are certain times when great care must be taken in treatment, and even times where treatment should not be administered. Fortunately for the patient, the scope of techniques available to the TCM practitioner is very wide. If one treatment avenue is blocked, there will probably be another that is open and available. Some of the more common cautions and contraindications for treatment with acupuncture, moxibustion, or other techniques are listed here:

➤ Ulcers or wounds are contraindicated for acupuncture and moxibustion. The patient can still receive treatment on other places of the body, but only if care is taken.

➤ Extreme hunger, fatigue and mental stress are not indicated for acupuncture and moxibustion.

➤ Pregnant women can be treated, but the practitioner must be very cautious.

➤ History of fainting during acupuncture treatments.

Acupuncture and moxibustion treatment must go together with dietary recommendations and lifestyle management.

(5) The effect of acupuncture on stroke

Now the mechanisms of acupuncture treatment for stroke has been basically explained.

➤ Acupuncture can promote the establishment of cerebral collateral circulation, accelerating the softening of thrombosis or blood clots, increasing cerebral blood circulation, and thereby promoting recovery of limb function[47].

➢ It can improve the blood supply to the brain, reducing brain tissue damage, which is conducive to the recovery of the motor skills[48,49].

➢ Acupuncture benefits the blood viscosity and agglutination[50,51].

➢ Acupuncture can significantly improve muscle strength, muscle tone, muscle flexibility, and the range of motion in joints for the stroke patient with spastic paralysis[52,53].

Therefore, as a treatment for stroke, acupuncture can not only improve cerebral blood flow, but also reduces morbidity, which shows a significant effect in clinic.

3. What Will Treatment Be Like?

After collecting detailed information (symptoms, signs, environment, tongue inspection, and pulse taking), the Chinese medical practitioner will identify the pattern of disharmonies present. Based upon this pattern identification, an optimal treatment protocol will be drawn up, according to theories of Chinese medicine.

The practitioner will then decide which modality (needles, moxa, cupping, etc.) to use during the present treatment. Usually needling is performed, and often one or more additional treatment modalities are used. The number and location of the needles is decided by the acupuncturist, and will probably vary from treatment to treatment, although some points will remain the same and begin to feel familiar. The points that remain the same are usually for your underlying root condition, while the points that change frequently are often to deal with whatever symptoms are most serious at the time of treatment. The amount of needles is not set, and can be as few as two or three or as many as thirty, but usually it is around ten to fifteen. The needles are mainly placed on the abdomen, back and limbs, with points on the scalp and face also used from time to time. The depth of the needle insertion is determined by the specific points, since the amount of flesh is different throughout the body. The length of needles is also decided by the acupuncturist, and usually is 0.5-1.5 inches (1.5-4.5 cm).

The needles are inserted quickly, at an angle of 15-90 degrees, in relation to the skin's surface. When an experienced acupuncturist inserts the needles, you normally will not feel any pain. The sensation is at most like being bitten by an ant. Acupuncture needles are much finer than

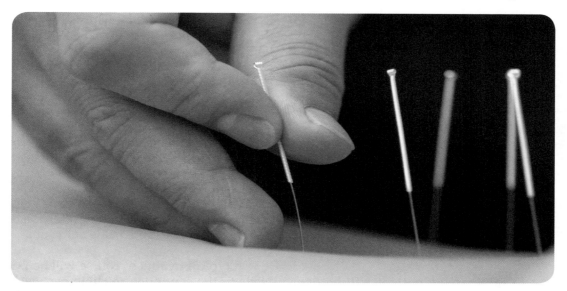

the hypodermic needles used in hospitals. But most importantly, trained acupuncturists can insert the needles quickly and correctly without causing unnecessary discomfort.

Once the needle has been inserted there are a variety of techniques like raising, thrusting, twirling, plucking and scraping, which strengthen the stimulation and sensation. The technique used will depend on the disease that is being treated. The patient is supposed to get a specific sensation called *dé qì*. *Dé qì* is a sensation specific to acupuncture treatment, and literally means "obtaining the qi". The exact feeling varies with each individual patient. There is not usually pain, but a unique sensation of soreness, heaviness, distension, tingling, or radiation in some direction. It is generally believed that the stronger the *dé qì* sensation is, the more effective the acupuncture treatment will be. After a few treatments, patients usually start to enjoy this sensation because it is both pleasant, and they know the good results it brings.

During treatment, it is best to relax and move as little as possible, unless the practitioner asks you to. Too much movement might cause the needles to bend, get stuck, or even break. These accidents are very rare, but if anything happens, stay calm and let the practitioner remove the needles immediately.

After the needles are inserted, the patient is usually left to relax for about 20–40 minutes. Other techniques such as moxa or cupping can be performed, before or after needling, depending on the practitioner. After the needles are removed, get up slowly and carefully. There is normally no bleeding during or after acupuncture treatment. If bleeding occurs, it will only be a few drops due to the breakage of small capillaries. Bruising is also very rare, but sometimes happens due to subcutaneous bleeding, also from broken capillaries.

After treatment, you will probably feel relaxed and energized. Some of your symptoms may disappear instantly. You may sleep better, have a more regulated appetite, feel less pain, or experience less anxiety.

In rare cases a patient will be over responsive to the treatment. This usually happens when a patient is extremely hungry, weak, nervous, or the stimulation and *dé qì* sensation is too strong. The patient might experience nausea, possibly vomiting, develop a very pale complexion, feel weak, sweat excessively, or even faint. If this happens, the acupuncturist will remove all the needles and allow the patient to lie down and rest for a while. Normally the patient will recover quickly. If the patient still feels unwell, a few points may be needled that will bring relief to the patient's symptoms.

It is advised to be in the best condition possible when you have your acupuncture treatments. Don't come for your acupuncture treatment when you are very hungry or just after a big meal, and try to be rested. Get the most out of your treatment by being extra careful of your general health the day before and after treatment. Help Chinese medicine help you!

A typical treatment course will be 2-3 visits to the acupuncture clinic per week for 4-8 weeks. After this the practitioner and patient will reevaluate, and decide on future treatment. Stroke rehabilitation is a chronic process, the treatment should not be rushed; it will often take several months of treatment. At the same time, doctor and patient commitment and good communication during treatment, can accelerate the speed of recovery.

4. Translated Research

Mei Lin-feng observed the effects of treating coma patients, resulting from cerebral hemorrhage, with scalp, auricular and body acupuncture combined with "sharpening the mind and inducing consciousness". Method: 56 coma patients were randomly divided into a multiple method group (36 cases) and a simple method group (20 cases). Results: The recovery rate in the multiple method group was 69.4%, and in the control group was 40%. There was a significant difference between multiple and simple therapy groups (P<0.05). Conclusion: The multiple methods with scalp, auricular and body acupuncture combined with "sharpening mind and inducing consciousness", is preferable to simple body acupuncture[54].

In order to study the auricular plaster and bleeding ear apex (ěr jiān, 耳尖) on blood lipid levels in patients with hyperlipoproteinemia, Liu Hai-tao conducted a clinical trial. Method: 104 patients with high blood lipids were randomly divided into 2 groups. The treatment group, with 52 patients, were treated with auricular pressure, and bleeding the point on the tip of the ear, whereas the control group, with 52 patients, were treated orally with probucol, twice a day. The treatment continued for 30 days. Results: The total effective rate was 92.31% in the treatment group, and 94.23% in the control group, the difference between the two groups being insignificant (P=0.314). The differences of serum TC, TG, HDL-CH and LDL-CH between the two groups, before and after treatment, were not significant (P>0.05). Conclusion: auricular-plaster combined with bleeding the tip of the ear for hyperlipoproteinemia is effective, easily accomplished, inexpensive and have clinical value[55].

Lu Hang-zhou carried out a study on animals, in order to observe the effects of auricular acupuncture on memory, hippocampus neuronal apoptosis, and the expression of apoptosis related protein enzyme-caspase-3 mRNA, in rats with vascular dementia (VD), and to explore the possible mechanisms of auricular acupuncture in the treatment of VD. Method: The vascular dementia model of rats was made by a 4-vessel blocking method; after auricular acupuncture had been given in the points of the brain and kidney, the learning and memory capability of rats was determined by morrismaze, and the TUNEL method was used to detect neuronal apoptosis in CA1 area of the rats' hippocampus, and the expression of caspase-3 mRNA was observed by situ hybridization. Results: The levels of neuronal apoptosis at CA1 area of hippocampus in the treatment group were significantly decreased (P>0. 01), and the expression of caspase-3 mRNA was also reduced, which was negatively correlated with the learning and memory abilities in the rats. Conclusion: Auricular acupuncture can improve the disorder of learning and memory abilities in rats with VD, and its action mechanism may be that acupuncture could depress the expression of caspase-3 mRNA, inhibit neuronal apoptosis, and protect the hippocampus neuron after cerebral ischemia[56].

Hu Jing-jing explored the effects of scalp acupuncture on intelligence in patients with vascular dementia (VaD) due to stroke (CI). Method: 68 patients were randomly divided into a scalp acupuncture treatment group, and a Western drug treatment group. A comparison was made before and after treatment by means of the mini mental status examination

(MMSE), the Blesse dementia scale (BDS), the Hasegawa dementia scale (HDS) and activity of daily living (ADL) score. Results: 61 patients completed the trial. MMSE, BDS and HDS scores increased and the ADL score decreased significantly in both groups after treatment (P<0.05). But there were no statistical significant differences in HDS, ADL, BDS and MMSE scores before and after treatment, or post treatment differences in the total efficacy rate between the two groups (P>0.05). Conclusion: Scalp acupuncture treatment can improve intellectual status to a certain degree, in patients with CI-caused VaD[57].

Cai Heng investigated the clinical efficacy of scalp acupuncture combined with body acupuncture, in treating postapoplectic hemiplegia. Method: 120 patients with postapoplectic hemiplegia were randomly divided into groups. 66 patients were designated to the scalp acupuncture plus body acupuncture group (group A), and 54 patients were designated to the conventional acupuncture group (group B). The clinical therapeutic effects were evaluated according to the global score of the patients' consciousness, language and limb function in the two groups. Results: In group A, a basic cure occurred in 6 cases, marked efficacy in 40 cases, and efficacy in 14 cases, with a total efficacy rate of 90.9%. In group B, a marked efficacy showed in 14 cases and efficacy in 22 cases, with a total efficacy rate of 66.7%. There was a statistically significant difference between the two groups (P<0.05). Conclu-

sion: The effect of scalp acupuncture plus body acupuncture is superior to that of conventional acupuncture, in treating the acute and restoration stages of stroke[58].

Lin Xiao-jun investigated the influence of concomitant scalp acupuncture and kinetotherapy, on somatosensory evoked potential (SEP) amplitude in patients with postapoplectic hemiplegia. Method: 48 patients with cerebral stroke were recruited and randomly divided into 2 groups. A treatment group of 24 patients, who received concomitant scalp acupuncture and kinetotherapy, and a control group of 24 patients who received kinetotherapy. After the treatment, SEP was used as an index for objective evaluation. The data was statistically analyzed. Results: There was no statistically significant before treatment difference in SEP N20 amplitude on the affected side, between the two groups (P>0.05). After treatment, SEP N20 amplitude on the affected side increased, and there was a statistically significant difference compared with before treatment, in both groups (P<0.01). There was a statistically significant difference after treatment in SEP N20 amplitude between the two groups (P<0.01). Conclusion: Concomitant scalp acupuncture and kinetotherapy are more effective than simple kinetotherapy, in restoring the cerebral function in patients with postapoplectic hemiplegia[59].

Wang Dao-hai observed the effects of acupuncture on different TCM syndrome types, in patients with apoplectic hemiplegia. Method: 57 patients with apoplectic hemiplegia were divided into qi deficiency with blood stagnation group (35 cases), and phlegm and blood causing blockages in the channels and collaterals group (22 cases). All patients were treated with scalp acupuncture combined with body acupuncture. The clinical therapeutic effect was evaluated according to the scores of manner, speech, motor function of limbs, and so on. Results: In the qi deficiency with blood stagnation group, 2 cases were cured, 17 showed marked efficacy, 12 showed efficacy, with a total effective rate of 88.6%. In the phlegm and blood causing blockages in the channels and collaterals group, 3 cases were cured,

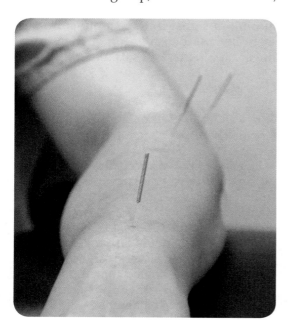

14 showed marked efficacy, 3 showed efficacy, with a total effective rate of 90.9%. There was a significant difference between the two groups in clinical remarkably effective rate (P<0.01), but no difference in total effective rate (P>0.05). Conclusion: Acupuncture can obviously improve consciousness, language, and limb function in patients with apoplectic hemiplegia. The effective rate of the pattern of phlegm and blood causing blockages in the channels and collaterals is more superior than the pattern of qi deficiency with blood stagnation[60].

In order to investigate the effect of the early intervention of scalp acupuncture, plus modern rehabilitation techniques, on motor functions and activities of daily living in patients with postapoplectic hemiplegia, Li Xiao-jun conducted a clinical trail. Method: A single blind randomized controlled trial was performed. 135 acute stroke patients, whose vital signs were stable and neurological signs no longer developing, were recruited. They were randomly divided into a scalp acupuncture rehabilitation group (45 cases), a rehabilitation group (45 cases), and a scalp acupuncture group (45 cases). Scalp acupuncture plus modern rehabilitation, simple modern rehabilitation, and simple scalp acupuncture were used separately for treatment. After 6 weeks of treatment, a statistical analysis was carried out using simplified Fugl-Meyer Assessment, the Barthel Index and the neurological deficit score as assessment criteria. Results: The Fugl-Meyer Assessment score and the Barthel Index score increased in all three groups of patients after 6 weeks of treatment, compared with before treatment; there was a statistically significant difference (P<0.01). After treatment, there were statistically significant differences in the Fugl-Meyer Assessment score and the Barthel Index score between the scalp acupuncture rehabilitation group, and the rehabilitation group, or the scalp acupuncture group (P<0.01). The cure and marked efficacy rate and the total efficacy rate were higher in the scalp acupuncture rehabilitation group, than in the rehabilitation group, and in the scalp acupuncture group (P<0.05). Conclusion: The early combined use of scalp acupuncture and modern rehabilitation, has a synergistic effect on postapoplectic hemiplegia, and can be a better protocol for the early convalescence of cerebral stroke patients[61].

Through observing the effects of acupuncture on cerebral function activities of patients with ischemic apoplexy, during finger movement using MRI, Wang Lina studied the relationship between acupuncture treatment and motor recovery of stroke patients, in order to provide a foundation for the therapeutic function of acupuncture[62].

Method: 15 patients with ischemic apoplexy and hand muscle strength were examined in a block design, by hemiparetic hand finger tapping, and finger tapping, with acupuncture at acupoints of LI 11 (qū

chí, 曲池), LI 10 (shǒu sān lǐ, 手三里), on the hemiparetic body. The dynamic T1 WI raw images were post-processed offline to form functional images. The distribution of brain function activation was analyzed. The size of the activation region, and the intensity of the signal were measured. Results: 15 subjects in both stimulus patterns were active in contralateral primary somatomotor area (Ml). In the finger tapping task, there were 4 subjects with contralateral premotor area (PMA), and 3 subjects with contralateral first somatosensory area (SI) activated. In the acupuncture task, there were 10 subjects with contralateral Ml, 7 subjects with contralateral S1, 2 subjects with ipsilateral Ml, and l subject with focus area and some other areas activated. The size of the activation region, and the minimum signal in the acupuncture task were both statistically larger than in the finger tapping task (P < 0.05).

Conclusion:

➢ It was feasible to explore the acupuncture mechanisms by using fMRI.

➢ These results showed the positive relationship between acupoints and brain functional regions.

➢ In the acupuncture task, ischemic apoplexy patient's fingers tapping could activate more intensively, and larger functional regions. This showed that acupuncture is a very useful treatment for recovery of movement in stroke patients.

Chinese Medicinals

1. What Are Chinese Medicinals?

(1) Introduction

"Chinese Medicinals" are the medicines based on TCM theory. They include Chinese crude medicine, prepared herbs from Chinese materia medica, traditional Chinese patent medicines, and simple preparations. Chinese herbology often incorporates ingredients from all parts of a plant, such as the leaf, stem, flower, and root, as well as using ingredients from animals and minerals.

Chinese Medicinals have been used for centuries. The first herbalist recorded in TCM theory is Shen Nong, a mythical person, who is said to have tasted hundreds of herbs and imparted his knowledge of medicinal and poisonous plants to farmers. The first Chinese manual of pharmacology is *Shen Nong's Classic of the Materia Medica* (*Shén Nóng Běn Cǎo Jīng*, 神农本草经), which lists about 365 medicines, of which 252 are herbs, and dates back somewhere in the 1st century of the Han dynasty. Earlier literature included lists of prescriptions for specific ailments, exemplified by a manuscript *"Recipes for 52 Ailments"*, found in the Ma Wang Dui Tomb, sealed in 168 B.C.

There is no doubt that the most important Chinese medical literature was *The Grand Compendium of Materia Medica* (*Běn Cǎo Gāng Mù*, 本草纲目), compiled during the *Ming* dynasty by Li Shi-zhen, which is still used today for consultation and reference. The history of this literature is presented in Paul U. Unschuld's *"Medicine in China: a History of Pharmaceutics"*; University of California Press, 1986.

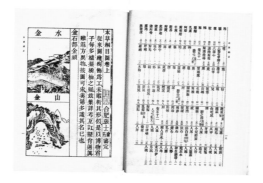

Herbology is one of the more important modalities utilized in TCM. Each herbal prescription is a cocktail of many herbs, tailored to suit the individual patient. One batch of herbs is typically decocted twice over the course of one hour. The practitioner usually designs a remedy using one or two main ingredients that target the illness. Then the practitioner adds many other ingredients, to adjust the formula to the patient's yin-yang conditions. Sometimes ingredients are needed to cancel out toxicity or side-effects of the main ingredients. Some herbs require the use of other ingredients as a catalyst or else the brew is ineffective. The latter steps require great experience and knowledge, and make the difference between a good Chinese herbal doctor and an amateur. Unlike western medications, the balance and interaction of all the ingredients are considered more important than the effect of the individual ingredients. A key to success in TCM is the treatment of each patient as an individual.

Chinese herbology can be used orally (that is, drunk) or externally, as in the case of medicated, herbal adhesive plasters applied to the skin in order to treat certain diseases.

(2) Mechanism of Chinese medicinals

The medical effect that Chinese Herbs plays on the human body is called action. The TCM theories believe that the human body in a healthy condition has normal activity within the organs and channels, balances yin and yang, and keeps a dynamic equilibrium with the outer environment. When various pathological factors influence the human body, the harmony and coordination of this balance are disrupted. When pathogens intensify and the healthy qi subsides, the yin, yang, qi and blood are disturbed, and the dysfunctions of the organs and channels develop into ailments. The appropriate utilization of Chinese herbs is aimed at specific pathogenesis directly, eliminating the pathogens, assisting healthy qi, coordinating organic action, and correcting the equilibrium of yin and yang to recover the human body, or restore the normal condition of balance. This is the basic effect of Chinese herbs.

The effects of Chinese herbs on the human body may be favorable or harmful. The same herb, when applied for the need of human physiological action or correction of pathological changes, is positive. But when it's used in an unnecessary situation, the herb will disturb or destroy

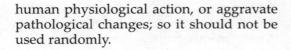

human physiological action, or aggravate pathological changes; so it should not be used randomly.

The basic principle of clinical medicinal application is to understand the overall effect and characteristics of Chinese herbs, use wisely, take advantage of therapeutic effects, avoid adverse effects, prevent toxic effects, and ensure the safety and effectiveness of the herbal remedy.

(3) Classification of Chinese herbs

Chinese physicians used several categorization methods to classify Chinese herbs:

➢ The four natures: this pertains to the degree of yin and yang, namely cold (extreme yin), cool, warm and hot (extreme yang). The patient's internal balance of yin and yang is taken into account when the herbs are selected. For example, medicinal herbs of "hot", yang nature are used when the person is suffering from internal cold that requires purging, or when the patient has a general cold constituency. Sometimes an ingredient is added to offset the extreme effect of one herb.

➢ The five tastes: the five tastes are pungent, sweet, sour, bitter, and salty, and each taste has a different set of functions and characteristics. For example, pungent herbs are used to generate sweating, and to direct and vitalize the qi and blood. Sweet tasting herbs often tonify or harmonize bodily systems. Some sweet tasting herbs also exhibit a bland taste, which helps drain dampness through diuresis. The sour taste most often is astringent or consolidates, while the bitter taste dispels heat, purges the bowels and eliminates dampness by drying it out. The salty taste softens hard masses, as well as purging and opening the bowels.

➢ The channels: the channels refer to which organs the herb acts upon. For example, mint is pungent, cool and is linked with the lungs and the liver. Since the lungs are the organ which protect the body from the invasion of cold and influenza, mint can help to purge the coldness from the lungs, and any invading heat toxins caused by hot "wind".

The earlier Materia Medica (*Běn Cǎo*), from the *Han* through *Tang* eras, began with a three level categorization:

➢ Low level: drastic acting, toxic substances
➢ Middle level: medicinal physiological effects
➢ High level: health and spirit enhancement

Proper selection of medicinals is the key to avoiding side effects. As they say, "One man's meat is another man's poison".

The use of medicinals is a complex process. Not only must the practitioner understand the individual properties of each substance, but also the relationship of substances when combined, contraindications, dosage and method of administration must all be properly understood. The effect of a medicinal can be strengthened, weakened, or even made toxic depending on what it is combined with.

In clinical practice, practitioners of Chinese medicine gradually form a number of basic prescriptions (usually called formulas in Chinese medicine) that fit the common patterns seen in each disease.

These formulas will be modified according to each specific case.

Traditional Chinese medicine has methods of nourishing qi and blood, suppressing hyperactive liver yang, relieving spasms by calming endogenous wind to expand the blood vessels, improving microcirculation and preventing thrombosis; regulating blood pressure and blood lipids, stopping bleeding, waking, and clearing obstructions in blood vessels and channels to help physical or language barriers and other functional recovery; as well as enhancing the body's resistance to disease, increasing immunity, and improving the patient's mood. It enables patients to treat and prevent further episodes of stroke. In general, medicinals used in stroke management are divided into four categories:

◆ **Blood activating and stasis resolving herbs**

The main actions of these herbs are dredging and facilitating blood vessels, promoting blood circulation, and resolving and eliminating blood stasis. They are usually indicated for blood stasis syndromes, and are called blood activating and stasis resolving herbs.

◆ **Liver pacifying and yang subduing herbs**

The main actions of these herbs are pacifying the liver and subduing yang.

They are indicated for liver yang hyperactivity due to liver and kidney yin deficiency, and yin deficiency with yang hyperactivity, with symptoms of dizziness, blurred vision, headaches, tinnitus, irritability, tendency to anger, insomnia, and dream-disturbed sleep. Some herbs also have combining actions of clearing liver heat and inducing calmness.

◆ Extinguishing wind and arresting convulsion herbs

The actions of these herbs are extinguishing wind and stopping spasms. The common symptoms of stroke are spasms and convulsions. Extinguishing wind and stopping spasms refers to the therapeutic actions for the stirring of liver wind, which is pacifying endogenous wind and stopping spasms.

◆ Tonifying deficiency herbs

The actions of these herbs are tonifying deficiency and rectifying weak conditions. These herbs also supplement yang, supplement qi, supplement blood, supplement yin, and can strengthen health and improve resistance to disease.

(4) Chinese medicinals in common use ♫

Chinese medicinals are very rarely used alone. But in order to construct a proper formula, the practitioner must be familiar with the properties of each individual herb. Since patients may present in any possible combination of patterns, any one of the thousands of medicinal substances may show up in a patient's formula. But as we have seen, there are a few main patterns that are typically present in stroke patients. And for each of these main patterns, there are certain medicinals that are most effective, and therefore most commonly used. In addition, due to scientific research, some herbs are known to be effective for stroke management. Below are some brief descriptions of some of the most commonly used medicinals in the treatment of stroke:

Huáng qí (黄芪, **Radix Astragali**)

Source: root of the perennial herbaceous plant

Property: sweet, warm

Functions: tonifies qi, raises yang, tonifies the defensive aspect to secure the superficial, relieves edema through diuretics, dispels toxins to promote skin regeneration, and nourishes blood. Astragalus root is effective for limb numbness in stroke patients, due to qi deficiency and blood stasis, as well as hemiplegia, and bedsores. It can enhance the body's resistance to disease and strengthen the immune system, which are conducive to stroke recovery.

Pharmacology studies: modern pharmacological studies have shown that astragalus saponins can inhibit platelet aggregation to combat thrombosis and prolong arterial thrombosis, improving local blood supply to the brain and protecting nerve cells. Astragalus can clear free radicals, combat the release of endothelin, significantly reduce neutrophil infiltration in ischemia reperfusion brain tissue, and thereby reduce cerebral ischemia and reperfusion inflammatory responses which play a role in cerebral protection.

Hóng huā (红花 **Flos Carthami**)

Source: dried flower of the annual herbaceous plant Carthamus tinctorius L. of family Compositae

Property: pungent, warm

Functions: activates the blood and dredges channels, dispels stasis, and alleviates pain.

Pharmacology studies: safflower contains flavonoids, safflower polysaccharides, organic acid, riboflavin and other ingredients. Experimental results show that safflower can prolong plasma recalcification time, prothrombin time, and thrombin time, significantly inhibit platelet aggregation and microcirculation, and has anticoagulant and antithrombotic effects. Used in traditional Chinese medicine to promote blood circulation, safflower extract provides beneficial results in the treatment of stroke patients.

Sān qī (三七, **Radix et Rhizoma Notoginseng)**

Source: root of the perennial herbaceous plant Panax notoginseng (Burk.) F.H.Chen. of family Araliaceae

Property: sweet, slightly bitter, warm

Functions: resolves blood stasis and stops bleeding, activates blood and alleviates pain. Notoginseng root is an important medicine for blood syndromes; it is able to remove stasis, and stop bleeding, which create significant effects in the treatment of acute cerebral hemorrhage.

Pharmacology studies: modern pharmacological studies have shown that notoginseng root is able to expand cerebral blood vessels, reduce cerebral vascular resistance, and increase cerebral blood flow. It can significantly reduce cerebral ischemia and reperfusion edema, as well as improving the blood-brain barrier permeability and local blood flow. Its function as a calcium channel blocker, enables it to reduce brain injury in the blood and malondialdehyde (MDA) content in brain tissue, which has the protective effect of traumatic brain injury; it has a sedative and analgesic effect; and could significantly increase SOD activity in brain tissue and blood, thus providing a preventative role in aging, and atherosclerosis.

Dān shēn (丹参, **Radix et Rhizoma Salviae Miltiorrhizae)**

Source: dried root and rhizome of the perennial herbaceous plant- salvia miltiorrhizain labiatae family

Property: bitter, slightly cold

Functions: activates the blood and

removes obstructions, cools blood and removes abscesses, relieves restlessness and induces calmness.

Pharmacology studies: danshen expands the peripheral vasculars, improves microcirculation, increases cerebral blood flow, promotes brain repair and regeneration of blood vessels, and inhibits thrombosis; it can inhibit the excessive proliferation of vascular endothelial cells and prevent arteriosclerosis. Therefore, danshen is very useful in the early treatment of stroke. In acute phases of cerebral hemorrhage, using danshan to cool blood and calm collaterals maintains stability

in patients, as well as improving blood supply to the brain, which is conducive to stroke recovery.

Tiān má (天麻, **Rhizoma Gastrodiae)**

Source: dried seed piece of family Orchidaceae

Property: sweet neutral

Functions: extinguishes wind and stops spasms, pacifies liver yang, dispels wind and unblocks collaterals.

Pharmacology studies: tall gastrodis tuber can be used to treat stroke due to hyperactive liver yang, and liver wind

moving, with the symptoms of dizziness, headaches, red face, limb numbness, and limb paralysis. It also has certain antihypertensive effects. Experimental studies have shown that tall gastrodis tuber can reduce peripheral vascular and coronary vascular resistance, lower blood pressure, sedate, prevent loss of consciousness, prevent inflammation, prevent aging, slow heart rate, relieve pain, improve learning and memory, and increase the immune function. In recent years, studies have found that it also has a beneficial effect on dementia in the elderly.

Chuān xiōng (川芎, Rhizoma Chuanxiong)

Source: dried rhizome of the perennial herbaceous plant Ligusticum chuanxiong

Property: pungent, warm

Functions: activates blood circulation and moves qi, expels wind and alleviates pain.

Pharmacology studies: *chuān xiōng* root extract TMP expands the small arteries, veins, and tissue ischemia, indirectly inhibits platelet aggregation and activation, increases cerebral blood flow and microcirculation, significantly reduces ischemic brain tissue damage, and improves the function of the nervous system. The TMP dendrite is able to protect and repair nerve cells and mitochondria, as well as protecting the brain tissue possibly through anti-free radical injury. TMP may extend time of ADP-induced platelet aggregation in outer vitro, and break down concentrated platelets, and inhibiting thrombosis.

Hé shǒu wū (何首乌, Radix Polygoni Multiflori)

Source: root tuber of the perennial twining plants of family Knotweed

Property: bitter, sweet, astringent, slightly warm

Functions: benefits the liver and kidney, nourishes qi and blood, and relaxes the bowels.

Pharmacology studies: according to modern pharmacological research, fleeceflower root decoction plays a large role in blood glucose levels. Its main component

is lecithin, which can promote the role and development of new blood cells. It has fibrinolytic activities, which enable patients with atherosclerosis to reduce thrombosis or micro-thrombosis; it contains anthraquinones (such as emodin), which have laxative effects, which is beneficial to treat age related constipation. It can be used for dizziness, insomnia, and poor memory caused by deficiency of the liver and kidney.

Shān zhā (山楂, Fructus Crataegi)

> **Source:** crataegus fruit
> **Property:** sour, sweet, warm
> **Functions:** Chinese hawthorn fruit

was also introduced in the chapter on diet. While this fruit lowers blood pressure and blood fats, its Chinese medical actions are more focused on the digestive system. It eliminates food stagnation, which often causes bloating, belching, and difficult bowel movements. It is a very commonly seen ingredient in many products in China. Bottled drinks are made from it, candy wafers given after meals contain it to help digestion, and in winter the whole fruit is prepared covered in hardened sugar; is a very tasty and popular treat.

Pharmacological studies: research has shown that hawthorn fruit contains lipase and numerous acids that promote the secretion of bile and stomach juices, to help the digestion of fats, particularly animal fat. Also, hawthorn fruit can lower blood pressure and levels of blood fat.

2. What Will Treatment Be Like?

Chinese herbs are the mainstay of Chinese medicine. Although acupuncture is the most recognized modality here in the West, in China the great majority of patients who seek treatment from Chinese doctors receive herbal formulas. Treatment with herbal medicine is thought to have a wider scope, than acupuncture, and for most diseases it works faster. The practical advantage of treatment with Chinese herbs, is the reduced number of clinic visits, making it more convenient for the patient. Acupuncture patients usually go to visit their doctors two or three times per week, while herbal prescriptions are usually modified once a week.

boiling raw herbs to extract their effective properties, and then drinking the liquid of the herbs. In TCM it is called "decoction". In general, taking Chinese herbs as a decoction is the most effective and quickest form of treatment.

Since treatment methods vary greatly from disease to disease, and styles differ between practitioners, the exact amounts of herbs, number of packets, and preparation instructions will be very different. Here we are trying to give a general idea about a typical treatment. If your practitioner gives you something that falls outside the guidelines listed here, do not be concerned.

(1) Preparation of the decoction ℘

Similar to the modalities that work on the points and channels, like acupuncture, moxibustion, and cupping, Chinese herbs can be administered in many different ways. The most common method is by

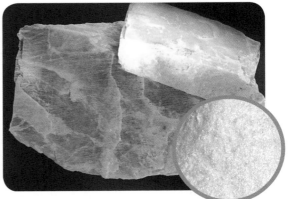

At the practitioner's clinic, you will most likely be given several packets of Chinese herbs. Each packet will be 1 day use, and will probably contain 70-120 g of herbs. Take the time to examine the herbs in the packet. Enjoy the different colors, smells, and textures. As many Chinese herbs are commonly seen plants in daily life, you may easily find some herbs that you are familiar with. Being able to get to know your medicine, and the ability to be involved in its preparation is one thing that never fails to endear a patient to Chinese herbs.

To cook the Chinese herbs, first put all of the herbs into a ceramic or glass pot (metal is not suitable), and add enough water to completely cover them (your doctor may tell you an exact amount of water to add). The mixture should be brought to the boil on a high heat, and then reduced to simmer on a medium heat. Typically the decoction needs to be cooked for 20-60 minutes, dependent upon the ingredients of the formula. When the decoction is cooked, strain and divide the liquid into two parts, drinking it twice a day in two equal portions, usually once after breakfast and once after dinner. One packet is usually one day's dosage. Sometimes you will be asked to save the herbs, to be cooked again in the future. In this case, they should be stored in the refrigerator. There are some ingredients that have particular cooking instructions: some herbs are cooked alone for 20-30 minutes before other ingredients are added (e.g. very dense herbs), some are added at the last five minutes of cooking (e.g very delicate herbs), and some are added last to the strained decoction (e.g materials in powder, gel, or liquid form).

Recently, some clinics have begun to offer a decoction cooking service. The decoction will be made by a machine and sealed in plastic bags to store in the refrigerator.

(2) Treatment course ♄

For chronic diseases, decoctions take time to have an effect. When you go to the clinic for the first time, the doctor will give a prescription for 3-7 days. Each day's dose should be divided into two equal parts, usually taken in the morning and evening. You will be required to return to the clinic after a week for the doctor to modify the prescription. After a month or so has passed, you and your doctor will reevaluate your condition, and your treatment strategy may change allowing for gradually smaller amounts of herbs. A treatment course usually lasts a few months, the time mainly depending on the severity of the case.

You are advised to take the decoction about one hour before or after meals. If the decoction irritates your stomach, take it after meals. The time may vary with the specific prescription, but generally speaking, it is common to take the decoction once in the morning before breakfast, and once at night before going to bed. Warm up the liquid before you drink it.

At first you may find the making of your decoction troublesome, and have a strong dislike of the unfamiliar taste. This is a common problem, especially in the west where we are accustomed to our medicine being easy to take, and either tasteless or sugar coated. We can only ask that you recall the millions of people who have benefited from this decoction treatment method, and give it a fair trial, at least two weeks. In fact, it is the experience of many doctors and patients that if the prescription properly fits the imbalance, the initially unfamiliar or unpleasant taste will become something the patient enjoys and looks forward to.

(3) Commonly used formulas

A typical formula consists of 5 to 15 ingredients, and the dosage of each ingredient is usually 6-30 g. The ingredients in the formula are arranged according to a hierarchy. The chief ingredient represents the main therapeutic effect, and will often have the largest dose. The assistants and deputies either support the chief, address another aspect of the imbalance, or perform a checking action against some other ingredient that may be too harsh in some way. The last soldier, the courier, serves to guide the formula to a certain body part, organ, or channel, or acts to harmonize the formula[63].

The following 6 types of patterns are commonly seen in clinical practice[64,65].

◆ **Pattern of ascending hyperactivity of liver yang**

Clinical manifestations: paroxysmal vertigo, paroxysmal unilateral numbness, temporary sluggish speech, temporary unilateral weakness and limpness, temporary double vision and dizziness, red complexion, distending pain in the head, red eyes, bitter taste in the mouth, restlessness and irritability, trembling limbs, reddish yellow urine, red tongue with a thin yellow coat or dry yellow coat, and a rapid string-like pulse.

Recommended formula and Chinese herbs: Modified *Tiān Má Gōu Téng Tāng* (天麻钩藤汤, Gastrodia and Uncaria Decoction)

Herbs	Pinyin	Dose	Latin Name
天麻	*tiān má*	10 g	Rhizoma Gastrodiae
钩藤	*gōu téng*	20 g	Ramulus Uncariae Cum Uncis
石决明	*shí jué míng*	15 g	Concha Haliotidis
黄芩	*huáng qín*	10 g	Radix Scutellariae
牛膝	*niú xī*	10 g	Radix Achyranthis Bidentatae
杜仲	*dù zhòng*	10 g	Cortex Eucommiae
益母草	*yì mǔ cǎo*	15 g	Herba Leonuri
桑寄生	*sāng jì shēng*	15 g	Herba Taxilli
山栀	*shān zhī*	10 g	Fructus Gardeniae

◆ **Pattern of phlegm heat obstructing the interior (yang blockage)**

Clinical manifestations: loss of consciousness, hemiplegia, deviated tongue, snoring and phlegm rale, contracture of the limbs, stiffness of the neck and fever, foul mouth odor, restlessness, even reversal cold of the extremities, frequent muscular twitching, occasional vomiting of blood, red and crimson tongue body with a yellow brown, slimy and dry coat, and a string-like, slippery, and rapid pulse.

Method of treatment: clears heat and resolves phlegm, and opens the orifices.

Recommended formula and Chinese herbs: Modified *Líng Yáng Jiǎo Tāng* (羚羊角汤, Antelope Horn Decoction)

Herbs	Pinyin	Dose	Latin Name
水牛角粉	*shuǐ niú jiǎo fěn*	20 g	Cornu Saigae Tataricae powder
石决明	*shí jué míng*	12 g	Concha Haliotidis
夏枯草	*xià kū cǎo*	15 g	Fructus Lycii
菊花	*jú huā*	15 g	Flos Chrysanthemi
龟板	*guī bǎn*	15 g	Plastrum Testudinis
生地	*shēng dì*	10 g	Radix Rehmanniae
丹皮	*dān pí*	15 g	Cortex Moutan

Herbs	Pinyin	Dose	Latin Name
白芍	*bái sháo*	10 g	Radix Paeoniae Alba
天竺黄	*tiān zhú huáng*	10 g	Concretio Silicea Bambusae
胆南星	*dǎn nán xīng*	10 g	Arisaema cum Bile

Recommended Chinese patent medicines:

Ān Gōng Niú Huáng Wán (安宫牛黄丸, Peaceful Palace Bovine Bezoar Pill). Take one pill, once a day, orally or by nasal feeding. For patients with severe conscious disturbance, take one pill, two or three times a day.

◆ **Pattern of phlegm obstructing the orifices (yin blockages)**

Clinical manifestations: loss of consciousness, hemiplegia, deviated tongue, phlegm rale, bright pale complexion with dusky lips, limp flaccid extremities, lying quietly without vexation, fecal incontinence and spontaneous urination, damp and cold body, dark purple tongue body with a white slimy coat, and a sunken, slippery and moderate pulse.

Method of treatment: dries dampness to resolve phlegm, and opens the orifices.

Recommended formula and Chinese herbs: Modified *Dí Tán Tāng* (涤痰汤, Phlegm Flushing Decoction)

Herbs	Pinyin	Dose	Latin Name
半夏	*bàn xià*	20 g	Rhizoma Pinelliae
制天南星	*zhì tiān nán xīng*	12 g	Rhizoma Arisaematis praeparatum
陈皮	*chén pí*	15 g	Pericarpium Citri Reticulatae
枳实	*zhǐ shí*	15 g	Fructus Aurantii Immaturus
茯苓	*fú líng*	15 g	Poria
人参	*rén shēn*	10 g	Radix et Rhizoma Ginseng
石菖蒲	*shí chāng pú*	15 g	Rhizoma Acori Tatarinowii
远志	*yuǎn zhì*	10 g	Radix Polygalae
甘草	*gān cǎo*	10 g	Radix et Rhizoma Glycyrrhizae
生姜	*shēng jiāng*	10 g	Rhizoma Zingiberis Recens

Recommended Chinese patent medicine:

Sū Hé Xiāng Wán (苏荷香丸, Sorax Pill), recorded in *Prescriptions from the Great Peace Imperial Grace Pharmacy*. Take one pill, two or three times a day, orally or by nasal feeding.

(4) Channel and collateral stroke

◆ **Pattern of wind phlegm obstructing the collaterals**

Clinical manifestations: hemiplegia, deviated tongue, sluggish speech or aphasia, hypoesthesia or sensory deprivation, dizziness and blurred vision, excessive sticky phlegm, dusky tongue body with a white slimy coat, and a string-like, slippery pulse.

Method of treatment: resolves phlegm to unblock collaterals

Recommended formula and Chinese herbs: Modified *Huà Tán Tōng Luò Tāng* (Phlegm Transforming and Collateral Unblocking Decoction)

Herbs	Pinyin	Dose	Latin Name
半夏	*bàn xià*	9 g	Rhizoma Pinelliae
白术	*bái zhú*	15 g	Rhizoma Atractylodis Macrocephalae
天麻	*tiān má*	15 g	Rhizoma Gastrodiae
丹参	*dān shēn*	15 g	Radix et Rhizoma Salviae Miltiorrhizae
香附	*xiāng fù*	15 g	Rhizoma Cyperi
胆南星	*dǎn nán xīng*	10 g	Arisaema cum Bile
酒大黄	*jiǔ dà huáng*	15 g	Radix et Rhizoma Rhei prepared with wine
三七	*sān qī*	17 g	Radix et Rhizoma Notoginseng

◆ **Pattern of phlegm heat and intestinal obstruction**

Clinical manifestations: hemiplegia, deviated tongue, sluggish speech or aphasia, hypoesthesia or sensory deprivation, abdominal distention and constipation, headache and blurred vision, expectoration or excessive phlegm, dark red tongue body with a yellow slimy coat, and string-like, slippery pulse, or string-like, slippery and large pulse in hemiplegia region.

Method of treatment: resolves phlegm to unblock bowels

Recommended formulas and Chinese herbs: Modified *Xīng Lóu Chéng Qì Tāng* (Bile Arisaema and Snakegourd Fruit Qi-Coordinating Decoction), recorded in *Treatise on Cold Damage Diseases*.

The dosage of rhubarb root and *máng xiāo* depends on the patient's constitution. Use with caution, do not overdose.

Herbs	Pinyin	Dose	Latin Name
全瓜蒌	quán guā lóu	20 g	Fructus Trichosanthis
胆南星	dǎn nán xīng	12 g	Arisaema cum Bile
大黄	dà huáng	15 g	Radix et Rhizoma Rhei
芒硝	máng xiāo	15 g	Natrii Sulfas

◆ **Pattern of qi deficiency with blood stasis**

Clinical manifestations: hemiplegia, deviated tongue, sluggish speech or aphasia, hypoesthesia or sensory deprivation, bright pale complexion, shortness of breath and weakness, salivation at corner of mouth, spontaneous sweating, palpitations, loose stools, swollen extremities, dusky tongue body with a thin, white coat with scallops, and a sunken and fine pulse.

Method of treatment: tonifies qi and activates blood

Recommended formula and Chinese medicinals: Modified *Bǔ Yáng Huán Wǔ Tāng* (补阳还五汤, Yang Supplementing and Five-Returning Decoction), recorded in *Correction of Errors in Medical Works* (*Yī Lín Gǎi Cuò*, 医林改错)[66].

Herbs	Pinyin	Dose	Latin Name
黄芪	huáng qí	20 g	Radix Astragali
当归	dāng guī	12 g	Radix Angelicae Sinensis
桃仁	táo rén	15 g	Semen Persicae
红花	hóng huā	15 g	Flos Carthami
赤芍	chì sháo	15 g	Radix Paeoniae Rubra
川芎	chuān xiōng	10 g	Rhizoma Chuanxiong
地龙	dì lóng	15 g	Pheretima

◆ **Pattern of yin deficiency with stirring wind**

Clinical manifestations: hemiplegia, deviated tongue, sluggish speech or aphasia, hypoesthesia or sensory deprivation, dizziness and tinnitus, heat in the palms and soles, dry pharynx and mouth, thin red tongue body with little or no coat, and a string-like, fine, and rapid pulse.

Method of treatment: enriches yin to extinguish wind

Recommended formula and Chinese medicinals: Modified *Zhèn Gān Xī Fēng Tāng* (镇肝息风汤, Liver-Sedating and Wind-Extinguishing Decoction)

Herbs	Pinyin	Dose	Latin Name
怀牛膝	*huái niú xī*	10 g	Radix Achyranthis Bidentatae
泽泻	*zé xiè*	10 g	Haematitum
龟板	*guī bǎn*	10 g	Plastrum Testudinis
白芍	*bái sháo*	15 g	Radix Paeoniae Alba
天冬	*tiān dōng*	15 g	Radix Asparagi
元参	*yuán shēn*	10 g	Raidix Scrophulariae
川楝子	*chuān liàn zǐ*	15 g	Fructus Toosendan
生麦芽	*shēng mài yá*	30 g	Fructus Hordei Germinatus
茵陈	*yīn chén*	15 g	Herba Artemisiae Scopariae
甘草	*gān cǎo*	10 g	Radix et Rhizoma Glycyrrhizae

The above formulas are all based on prescriptions that were first put together hundreds, if not thousands, of years ago. In Chinese medicine, doctors build on the experience of the past, using formulas that have been proven to be effective. However, genius lies not only in the past, and many skilled doctors of the present have distilled their wisdom and experience into new formulas, to pass on to future generations of doctors.

(5) Other therapeutic forms of Chinese herbs ♺

In addition to Chinese herbal medicine for oral use, there are many other forms of therapy in Chinese medicine. Some methods are very simple; after the consultation with the doctor, it is optional to use at home.

◆ **Fumigation treatment**

Fumigation therapy is an external

herbal therapy, of washing the affected part with the warm herbs; the herbs are boiled into a soup, which is then applied onto the affected part, for heat treatment of fumigation and washing. Fumigation treatment is suitable for rehabilitation of affected limbs in stroke. Fumigation treatment uses the effects of temperature, pharmaceutical and machinery factors. This therapy increases blood circulation and warms the channels to alleviate pain. It is beneficial for the rehabilitation of affected limbs to boil soup, and then use the heated soup on the affected part for fumigation and washing. Due to the heat the blood vessels expand, which promotes blood circulation and improves local blood supply to the affected limbs. Method: place the heated soup in a bowl with hand or foot on it, put cloth to cover it and then begin to dip and steam. When the soup is no longer hot, and then put hand or foot soak in it for washing. Fumigation formula for treatment of affected limbs after stroke:

Herbs	Pinyin	Dose	Latin Name
桂枝	*guì zhī*	10 g	Ramulus Cinnamomi
当归	*dāng guī*	10g	Radix Angelicae Sinensis
乳香	*rǔ xiāng*	10 g	Olibanum
没药	*mò yào*	10 g	Myrrha
木瓜	*mù guā*	30 g	Fructus Chaenomelis

Herbs	Pinyin	Dose	Latin Name
透骨草	tàu gǔ cǎo	30 g	Raidix Scrophulariae
丹参	dān shēn	30 g	Radix et Rhizoma Salviae Miltiorrhizae
川芎	chuān xiōng	15 g	Rhizoma Chuanxiong
黄芪	huáng qí	30 g	Radix Astragali
威灵仙	wēi líng xiān	30 g	Radix et Rhizoma Clematidis
伸筋草	shēn jīn cǎo	30 g	Herba Lycopodii

Cassia twig 10 g, angelica 10 g, frankincense 10 g, myrrh 10 g, papaya 30 g, tuberculate speranskia herb 30 g, red sage root 30 g, chuanxiong root 15 g, astragalus 30 g, clematis root 30 g, common clubmoss herb 30 g.

◆ **Medical pillow therapy**

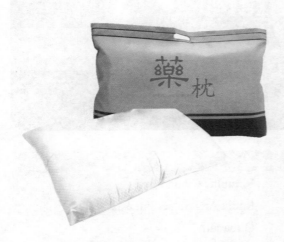

Approximately one third of a day is spent in bed. Pillows are essential components for sleeping. Using pillows properly not only helps sleep quality, but also plays a role in healthcare. It was discovered in ancient China that using a pillow filled with herbs (medicinal pillow) can prevent and even treat, many chronic diseases.

The mechanism of its role is multifaceted. Aromatic herbs can be selected for their functions: herbs that revive, calm, remove obstruction in the collaterals and channels; pungent herbs that stimulate the points on the head; herbs that enter the body through the skin pores and passages, to remove blockages in the blood, and balancing the qi in the body[67,68]. Secondly, the body temperature of the head and neck during sleep prompts the pharmaceutical ingredients in the pillow, to release slowly in the form of particles, which have slow and long lasting effects of lowering and regulating blood pressure. It has significantly improved headaches, dizziness, tinnitus, insomnia, forgetfulness, chest tightness and other symptoms, and is also beneficial in stroke sequelae[69].

Cassia chrysanthemum pillow 1500 g of white chrysanthemum (or wild chrysanthemum), and 1000 cassia seeds are required to make a medicinal pillow. The effect of the pillow helps to suppress hyperactive liver, to clear fire, improve eyesight, lower blood pressure; the pillow is good for preventing stroke caused by liver "yang".

Medicinal pillows are a commonly used therapy in the treatment of stroke patients; they are easy to make, easy to use, and are very effective.

◆ **Externally applied agent**

Bedsores result because stroke patients are often restricted to bed long-term, especially elderly, malnourished patients. The point at which the body touches the bed causes reduced flow of qi and blood, resulting in undernourished skin and muscles, and even necrosis, which leads to bedsores. Mild cases can be cured by suitable nursing care and treatment, while severe cases with ulceration are very difficult to try and cure. The external treatment is mainly applied in the local area when treating bedsores, and skin nursing should be emphasized.

For the pattern of internal accumulation of toxic heat, it manifests as dull purple skin or ulceration in the local area, rotting flesh, pus, foul smell, red tongue with little coat, and fine, rapid pulse. It is treated with *Rǔ Yì Jīn Huáng Gāo* (As One Wishes Golden Yellow Paste), by plaster-

ing it on the affected area. Change dressings every 6 to 12 hours.

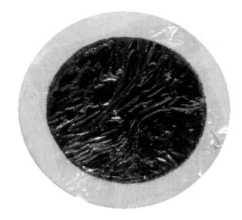

For the pattern of qi and blood deficiency, it manifests as necrotic tissue, or new tissue that is pale and slow to heal, pale tongue with little coat, and a thin, sunken, forceless pulse. It is treated with *Huó Xuě Shēng Jì Gāo* (Blood-Activating and Flesh-Engendering Paste), by plastering it on the affected area.

◆ **Chinese patent medicine**

Chinese patent medicine is part of traditional Chinese medicine. They are standardized herbal formulas. Several herbs and other ingredients are dried and ground. They are then mixed into a powder and formed into pills. Honey is traditionally used to bind all the ingredients together. They are characteristically little round black pills.

Chinese patent medicines are easy and convenient. They are not easy to customize on a patient-by-patient basis, however. They are best used when a patient's condition is not severe, and the medicine can be taken as a long-term treatment.

These medicines are not "patented" in the traditional sense of the word. No one has exclusive rights to the formula. Instead, "patent" refers to the standardization of the formula. All Chinese patent medicines of the same name will have the same proportions of ingredients.

Recommended Chinese patent medicines

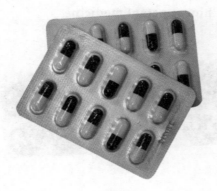

◆ Activating blood circulation to dissipate blood stasis

Tōng Xīn Luò Jiāo Náng (Freeing Heart Network Vessels Capsule). Take 1-4 pills, three times a day.

Nǎo Xīn Tōng Jiāo Náng (Freeing Network Vessels of the Brain and Heart Capsule). Take 4 pills, three times a day.

◆ Eliminating phlegm by cooling and dissipating phlegm for resuscitation

Ān Gōng Niú Huáng Wán (Peaceful Palace Bovine Bezoar Pill). Take 1 pill, once a day, orally, or by nasal feeding. For patients with severe conscious disturbance, take 1 pill, two or three times a day.

Niú Huáng Qīng Xīn Wán (Bovine Bezoar Heart Clearing Pill). Take 1-2 pills, twice a day, orally or by nasal feeding.

3. Translated Research

A Meta-analysis on randomized controlled trials (RCTS) of *Tōng Xīn Luò Jiāo Náng* (Freeing Heart Network Vessels Capsule) in the treatment of cerebrovascular disease was conducted to evaluate its efficacy and safety. A total of 37 articles of randomized controlled studies were investigated. It showed that there was a statistically significant difference in the total effective rate between the *Tōng Xīn Luò Jiāo Náng* (Freeing Heart Network Vessels Capsule) group and the control group, through analyzing 3,336 cases. In neurological deficit score, doing subgroup analysis according to disease classification, the studies on the treatment of acute stroke, showed that there was a statistically significant difference between the two groups. Very few adverse reactions, and no obvious side effects, occurred[70].

Nǎo Xīn Tōng Jiāo Náng (Freeing the Brain and Heart Network Vessels Capsule) is indicated for the treatment of the pattern of qi deficiency and blood stasis of ischemic stroke, at the convalescence stage. 80 patients were divided into the treatment group of *Nǎo Xīn Tōng Jiāo Náng* (Freeing Brain and Heart Network Vessels Capsule), and the control group of *Tōng Xīn Luò Jiāo Náng* (Freeing Heart Network Vessels Capsule), in a randomized double-blind placebo controlled trial. After four weeks treatment, the results showed that the treatment group of *Nǎo Xīn Tōng Jiāo Náng* (Freeing Brain and Heart Network Vessels Capsule) was superior to the control group, in improving patient's ability to participate in life, reducing blood fat, improving blood quality, and other aspects. There was a statistically significant difference between them[71].

It was reported by the Chinese Emergency Cooperation Group of Stroke in 1993, that herbal granules to pacify the liver and extinguish wind, transform phlegm and free the collateral vessels, transform phlegm and free the bowels, and tonify qi and activate blood, as well as ointments to nourish yin and extinguish wind, were applied in the treatment of 115 cases of acute stroke. 69 random patients were selected for the western medicine control group, and received dextran-40. Clinical observations and experimental research on the above series of formulas and medicinals in the treatment of stroke were carried out. Results showed that for the treatment group, the near recovery rate was 35.7%, the significantly effective rate was 35.7%, the total effective rate was 87.8%; for the control group, the near recovery rate was 17.4%, the significantly effective rate was 7.2%, the total effective rate was 71%. The curative effects of the above formulas and medicinal series were more effective than the western medicine dextran-40, and the differences between them were significant. Animal experimental research results showed that the formulas and medicinals above inhibited platelet aggregation, enhanced fibrinolytic activity, and prolonged thrombus formation in vivo to different degrees[72,73].

On the basis of the previous research results, China developed a comprehensive protocol for the treatment of stroke at the acute stage, with the characteristics of pattern identification and treatment, and carried out a multi-center clinical validation and evaluation study. A total of 522 cases of acute stroke patients were observed, in the follow up of 3 days, 7 days, 14 days, 28 days and 3 months after the disease onset. The neurological function, TCM patterns, and activities of daily living, cognitive function, quality of life and other aspects were comprehensively evaluated. The randomized controlled study on comprehensive treatment protocol of stroke, showed that on the 14th day after the disease onset, the effective rate of the combined therapy group was 77.1%, while the effective rate of the western medicine treatment group was 60.1%. There was a statistically significant difference between them[74,75].

In 1995, a randomized controlled study on treatment of 62 stroke patients with Hua Tan Tong Fu Tang (Transforming Phlegm and Freeing the Bowels Decoction), and Hua Tan Tong Luo Tang (Transforming Phlegm and Freeing the Collateral Vessels Decoction) was made, and dextran-40 was used for the control group. The findings showed that the curative effects of Hua Tan Tong Fu Tang (Transforming Phlegm and Freeing the Bowels Decoction) and Hua Tan Tong Luo Tang (Transforming Phlegm and Freeing the Collateral Vessels Decoction) were more effective than dextran-40 in the treatment of channel and collateral stroke in ischemic stroke[76,77].

Qīng Nǎo Tōng Luò Piàn (Spirit-arousing and Freeing the Collateral Vessels Tablet), whose main ingredients are danshen and cassia seed, was used orally to treat 301 cases of stroke prodrome, compared with 101 cases in the western medicine group, and the results showed that this medicinal had significant effects on relieving the prodromes of stroke and improving blood rheological characteristics; the total effective rate reached 86%, which was much more effective than that of the western medicine control group[78].

In 2002, a randomized control study on 240 cases of acute ischemic stroke was conducted, and the results indicated that the total effective rate of the treatment group, using the method of transforming phlegm and freeing the bowels was 91.9%, the marked effective rate was 73.3%; the total effective rate of the control group was 69.1%, the marked effective rate was 38.3%. The neurological deficits score and hemorrheological indexes, of the group using the method of transforming phlegm and freeing the bowels, were also better than those of the control group[79].

Tui Na (Massage)

1. What Is Tui Na?

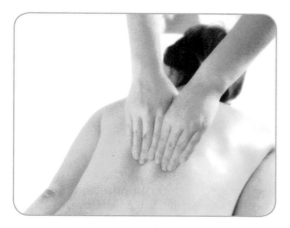

Tui na is a form of Chinese manipulative therapy, often used in conjunction with acupuncture, moxibustion, fire cupping, Chinese herbalism, tai ji, and qi gong. Tui na is a hands-on body treatment, designed to bring the body into balance. The principles of balance are the eight principles of TCM. The practitioner may brush, knead, roll, press, and rub the areas between each of the joints, to open the body's defensive qi and increase the movement of energy through both the channels and the muscles. The practitioner can then use range of motion, trac-

tion, and massage, with the stimulation of acupressure points, to treat both acute and chronic musculoskeletal conditions, as well as many non-musculoskeletal conditions. Tui na is an integral part of TCM, and is also related to Chinese massage or anma.

Chinese massage has a long history and dates back to the ancient times. As early as the New Stone Age, around 2700 B.C., the Chinese ancestors primarily summed up their primitive experiences in massage. This turned the spontaneous medical behavior that originated from self-defence instinct, into a medical mode for the early human race. Tui na has fewer side effects than modern drug-based and chemical-based treatments. It has been used to treat, or complement, the treatment of many conditions; musculo-skeletal disorders, and chronic stress related disorders of the digestive, respiratory, and reproductive systems.

In the treatment of stroke, tui na is effective, although it often plays a supplementary role. Manual stimulus on the acupuncture points (acupressure) also produces similar effects to that of acupuncture, according to the theory of TCM. Tui na is more convenient, and may also sound more appealing if you are afraid of needles. What's more important is that it is at least as effective as needles.

2. What Will Treatment Be Like?

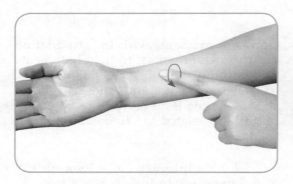

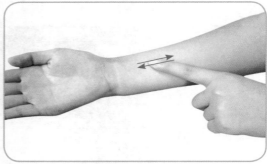

Application of the Chinese massage method has enriched the recovery training method. It is applied following the treatment, and the various techniques used increase the entire joint activity, alleviate aches, suppress convulsions, and assist passive movements. It is important to avoid strong stimulation to the convulsion muscle group, when treating patients with hemiparalysis. The massage techniques rub, pinches the law commonly used, also may coordinate other techniques. A pair of trained hands is all that is necessary for a tui na treatment to be performed. That is why the manipulations are called "shǒu fǎ" (techniques of the hands) in Chinese. Other parts of the practitioner's body may also be used, such as elbows and arms.

"Manipulation" is the key to tui na treatment. Its manipulating quality, and standard of its clinical differentiation, can directly affect the curative result of massage. Traditional massage requires that manipulation should be permanent, forceful, even and soft, so as to be deep and thorough. "Permanence" is that manipulation should last for a certain period of time according to the requirement, that is, the structure of manipulation keeps unchanged within a certain period of time and has a steady dynamic form. "Forcefulness" is that manipulation must have a certain force which should be strengthened or weakened, according to the patient's constitution, state of illness, age, and therapeutic portions. "Evenness" is that manipulation should be rhythmical, with the same frequency and pressing force all the time. "Softness" is that manipulation should be light, but not superficial, heavy but not retained, not rough and hard, and the shift of the movements should be natural and smooth. "Deepness and thoroughness" means that manipulation must keep a certain direction of force, in addition to the requirements above, in order to achieve a deep effect on the affected part of the patient's body and create a curative effect.

3. At–home Massage

Tui na increases the blood supply, oxygen, and nutrition to muscles, tissues, joints, and the vital organs, and improves circulation throughout the body. This helps muscles to recover more quickly from exertion and fatigue (especially useful after a strenuous workout), and helps to relieve the pain and discomfort associated with muscle tension, fractures, sprains, sciatica, and stiff joints.

Tui na therapy aids in the relief of muscle spasms and cramping, and helps in the prevention of muscular atrophy. Tui na therapy also helps break up scar tissue, and is especially useful in the breakup of post surgical adhesions and edema. It promotes a greater range of motion in joints, and keeps ligaments and tendons supple. It lowers blood pressure and heart rate, and reduces stress, anxiety, and even depression. As tui na helps reduce not only physical, but mental stress, it is often recommended as part of a regular program for stress management.

Tui na manipulation is actually a set of highly skilled techniques and expert movements that are performed according to TCM theory. It is targeted at the system of channels, and acupuncture points, throughout the body. Therefore, the manipulation must be performed by trained practitioners to promote internal self-adjustments of the channel system, without harming the local tissues of the body. The effect of tui na depends more on the skill with which the manipulations are performed, rather than on the sheer force of pressure. Force, even a small amount, applied improperly can be harmful to the body. It is not suggested that you perform or receive tui na treatments that you have observed in the clinic, on or by your friends or family members, without the presence of an instructor.

Nonetheless, there are some self massage practices which are safe, simple, convenient, and designed for stroke patients to exercise their body and mind, regulate organ function, and serve as a supplement to stroke management. There are many benefits to massage of which you may not be aware. At the stroke convalescence stage, or the sequela stage, patients may choose the following techniques, according to clinical need, such as rubbing, brushing, kneading, rolling, and so on.

The massage treatment of stroke has the bidirectional adjustment (including dissolve hitch, hematischesis) affects, eliminates the neck blood vessel of brain convulsion solvableand reduces the cerebrospinal fluid pressure and so on. The following is an introduction of stroke massage methods.

(1) Acting principle of massage

➢ Regulating yin and yang.

➢ Regulating the function of channels, collaterals, qi, blood and viscera.

➢ Recovery of the function of tendons, bones and joints.

➢ Relaxing muscles and tendons, and dredging the channels and collaterals.

➢ Restoring and treating injured soft tissues and reducing dislocated joints.

(2) Massage step

Firstly, massage the patient's shoulder, neck, and face, and then press the lower back region, and finally press down the lower limbs and into the chest and abdomen. Massage pressure should increase from light to heavy, step by step.

(3) Frequency

One hour massage once a day.

(4) Manipulation

Patient who has been ill within the past week; begin in supine position with the head and upper body slightly higher than the lower extremities; then change to side position, and seated position.

(5) Tui na on the head and neck

The head and neck massage:

➢ Fingers can be used on patients when massaging the shoulder and neck, focusing on the trapezius and related acupoints of the *du mai*, the foot *taiyang* bladder channel, the hand *yangming* large intestine channel, and the hand *shaoyang sanjiao* channel

➢ Massage, using your fingers, the patient's shoulder and neck muscles, as well as BL 10 (*tiān zhù*, 天柱), DU 15 (*yǎ mén*, 哑门), GB 20, GB 21 (*jiān jǐng*, 肩井), RN 23 (*lián quán*, 廉泉), and other points.

➢ Facial massage using your fingers on the patients' head and face muscles, as well as DU 20, DU 22 (*xìn huì*, 囟会), EX-HN 3 (*yìn táng*, 印堂), EX-HN 5 (*tài yáng*, 太阳), and DU 26 (*shuǐ gōu*, 水沟).

(6) Tui na on the back

Massage the back, around the waist, using the fingers to press into the erector spinae, quadratus lumborum, spine, and associated the acupoints of the *du mai*, and foot *taiyang* bladder channel.

(7) Tui na on the upper limbs

Massage the upper limbs, using the fingers to press into the limb muscles, as well as LU 3 (*tiān fŭ*, 天府), PC 3 (*qū zé*, 曲泽), LI 10, SJ 5 (*wài guān*, 外关), PC 6 (*nèi guān*, 内关), and LI 4.

(8) Tui na on the lower limbs

Massage the lower limbs, using the fingers to press into the lower limb muscles as well as SP 10 (*xuè hăi*, 血海), ST 36, BL 40 (*wĕi zhōng*, 委中), and KI 1.

(9) Tui Na on the chest

Knead the patient's abdominal muscles, as well as RN 20 (*huá gài*, 华盖), RN 18 (*yù táng*, 玉堂), RN 17 (*dàn zhōng*, 膻中), RN 12 (*zhōng wăn*, 中脘), ST 25 (*tiān shū*, 天枢), and RN 6 (*qì hăi*, 气海).

4. Self Treatment with Tui Na

(1) DU 20

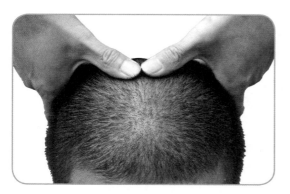

Location: 5.0 *cun* directly above the midpoint of the posterior hairline, or at the midpoint of the line connecting the apexes of the two auricles.

Indications: headache, dizziness, forgetfulness, apoplexy, manic disorder, and epilepsy.

Manipulation: the right hand, with thumb slightly curved, rubs and presses DU 20 for 2 times.

(2) LI 4

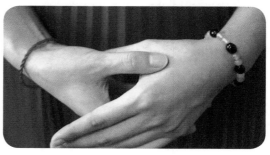

Location: on the dorsum of the hand, between the 1st and 2nd metacarpal bones on the radial side.

Indications: geadache, dizziness, redness, pain and swelling of the eye, and persistent turbid nasal discharge.

Manipulation: keep elbows relaxed with both palms down, and knead 40-80 times.

(3) LI 10 ♋

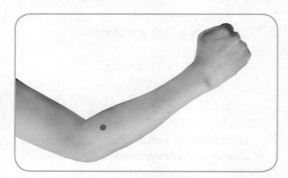

Location: on the dorsal radial side of the forearm, on the line connecting LI 5 (*yáng xī*, 阳溪), and LI 11, 2 *cun* below the transverse cubital crease.

Indications: abdominal distention, diarrrhea, toothache, and hoarse voice.

Manipulation: using the right hand thump the left elbow at LI 10, 40-80 times, and repeat on opposite side.

(4) PC 6 ♋

Location: on the palmar aspect of the forearm, 3 *cun* above the transverse crease of the wirst, on the line connecting PC 3

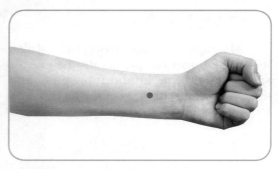

and PC 7 (*dà líng*, 大陵), between the tendons of m. palmaris longus and m. flexor carpi radialis.

Indications: cardiac pain, palpitations, chest pain, chest congestion, insomnia, and dizziness.

Manipulation: right thumb presses on the left inner forearm, at PC 6 for 2 minutes, and repeat on opposite side.

(5) LI 11 ♋

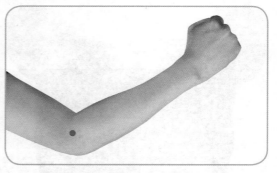

Location: when the elbow is flexed, the point is on the lateral end of the transverse cubital crease, at the midpoint between LU 5 (*chǐ zé*, 尺泽), and the lateral epicondyle of the humerus.

Indications: pain and swelling of the arm, numbness of the upper extremities, weakness of the hand and elbow, and abdominal pain.

Manipulation: slightly curve right thumb, and knead the left LI 11 for 2 minutes, and repeat on the opposite side.

(6) DU 4 (*mìng mén*, 命门) ♫

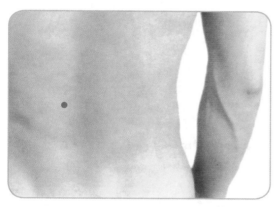

Location: In the depression below the spinous process of the second lumber vertebra.

Indications: lumbar pain with deficiency, urine retention, urinary frequency, and irregular menstruation.

Manipulation: right hand knocks on the DU 4, 40-80 times, and repeat with the left hand.

(7) RN 6 ♫

Location: on the anterior median line of the lower abdomen, 1.5 cun below the umbilicus.

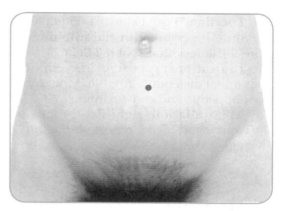

Indications: constipation, prolonged diarrhea, urine retention, urinary infection, urine retention, emissions, lower abdominal pain, and dysmenorrhea.

Manipulation: overlap the hands, and palm presses down on RN 6, for 2 minutes, overlap hands the opposite way and repeat.

(8) ST 36 ♫

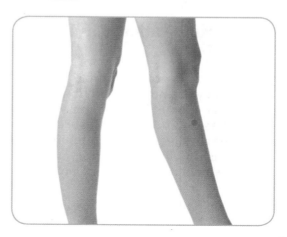

Location: 3 *cun* below ST 35 (*dú bí*, 犊鼻), one finger-breadth (middle finger), from the anterior crest of the tibia.

Indications: gastric pain, vomiting, abdominal distention, rumbling intestines, poor appetite, and constipation.

Manipulation: right fist thumps on the right leg at ST 36, repeat on the opposite leg.

(9) LV 3 (*Tài Chōng*, 太冲)

Location: on the dorsum of the foot, in a depression distal to the junctions of the first and second metatarsal bones.

Indications: headache, dizziness, redness, swelling and pain of the eye, and infantile.

Manipulation: right heel taps the left foot at LV 3, 40-80 times, and repeat on the opposite side, for 20 mins, twice a day. Two months comprises a course of treatment.

5. Contraindications for Tui Na

So far as contraindications are concerned, they are not absolute in massage therapy. For some diseases, massage can be used as an auxiliary measure, to increase the curative effect and eliminate the symptoms. In clinical practice, attention should be paid to the following points:

➢ Massage should not be used to treat motion organ disease due to tuberculin and pus organism. Massage is not suitable for cancer patients.

➢ Massage is not used in dermatological conditions with pathological changes, or when injuries, bruises and burns.

➢ Massage should be avoided on areas that are bleeding.

> Dislocations should be mainly treated with taxis.

> Massage should not be applied on the abdomen or lumbosacral areas in preg-nant women, or those who are menstruat-ing.

> Be cautious of fainting in patients who are hungry, or after strenuous exercise.

Case

In Beijing, Zou Yi-huai studied the effects of Chinese medicine foam wash and massage, for specific treatments, in a control group, over a course of treatment. Results showed that the "recovery Ton-gluo liquid", the Chinese medicine foam wash, alleviated shoulder-hand syndrome caused by pain, and local swelling, and that massage effectively alleviated spasms, and provided rehabilitation training.

6. Translated Research

Xing ying conducted a randomized control trial on the influence and mecha-nism of manipulation on the delayed onset of muscle soreness after extreme ex-ercise. Objective: To observe and compare the influences of pre and post exercise ma-nipulation, and natural recovery, without any intervention on delayed onset muscle soreness (DOMS) after extreme exercise, as well as exploring the manipulation therapeutic mechanism on the metabolism of oxygen free radical (OFR). Method: The 30 healthy male students were divided into 3 groups randomly, according to con-dition equivalence principle including pre exercise manipulation group (A), post ex-ercise manipulation group (B), and control group (C). Group A received manipulation for 30 minutes before beginning exercise 5 minutes later. Group B received manipula-tion for 30 minutes, 30 minutes after they had finished exercising. This continued once a day, for consecutive 3 days. Group C did not receive any manipulations, ei-ther before or after exercise. The clinical manifestations, which included soreness intensity and duration, maximal isometric strength, arm girth, and elbow range of motion were evaluated in the hour before exercise, immediately after exercise, and then 24, 48 and 72 hours after exercise. Serum creatine kinase (CK), serum su-peroxide dismutase (SOD), and serum malonaldehyde (MDA) were measured in the hour before exercise, immediately after exercise, and then 24 and 48 hours after exercise. Results: Compared to group C, group A and B showed significantly lower peak soreness (P<0.01, P<0.05), significantly better recovery of elbow flexing degree at 72 hours after exercise (P<0.05) and significantly lower rising range of serum CK at 48 hours after exercise (P<0.01). Compared to group C, group A showed significantly shorter duration of muscle soreness (P<0.0), and significantly better recovery of maximal iso-metric strength at 72 hours after exercise (P<0.01). Compared to group C, group B showed significantly better recovery of elbow extending degree at 72 hours after exercise (P<0.01). There was no significant difference in the change of arm girth among the three groups. The level of Serum SOD, MDA and SOD/MDA at 48 hours after exercise, in group A and B, were significantly different from those in group C (P<0.01, P<0.01, P<0.05, P<0.01). Conclusion: Through improving the metabolism of OFR, pre exercise and post exercise manipulation can partially prevent and treat DOMS respectively. In addition, the preventative effects of receiving manipulation before exercise is more beneficial than curing post exercise effects through manipulation; this proves the TCM thought, that is, prevention is superior to treatment[80].

Mr Li studied the effects on the functional recovery of hemiplegic limbs through early treatment. 60 patients were treated using acupuncture and western medicine simultaneously, and 30 patients received massage therapy with the main point of enamel rubbed France France accordance with the law and to take a day a time for each operation time about 30 minutes to restore limb edema and paralysis in the limb muscle spasticity improvements, than those in the control group there was significant difference in that the direct effect of skin and muscle massage techniques so that the mechanical energy into heat energy to increase the promotion of local skin and muscle capillary expansion of the nutrient supply to muscle atrophy can be improved at the same time ease the spasm elimination of edema[81].

Zhou Yan-ping explored the effects of Chinese medicine foot soaks and auricular plasters on insomnia in 80 patients. Method: Herbal powders for different syndromes were added into a foot basin (wooden basin, electronic massage basin) for the immersion of both feet, in conjunction with an auricular plaster, to discover the effects of treating and nursing insomnia. Results: of all the 80 cases, 69 cases cured, 9 cases improved, 2 cases failed, with the total effective rate of 97.5%. Conclusion: Traditional Chinese Medicine therapy of foot soaks in conjunction with auricular plasters, has the advantages of obvious curative effects, it is a simple procedure, easily accepted by patients, and has no side effects; which is an effective method in the treatment of insomnia[82].

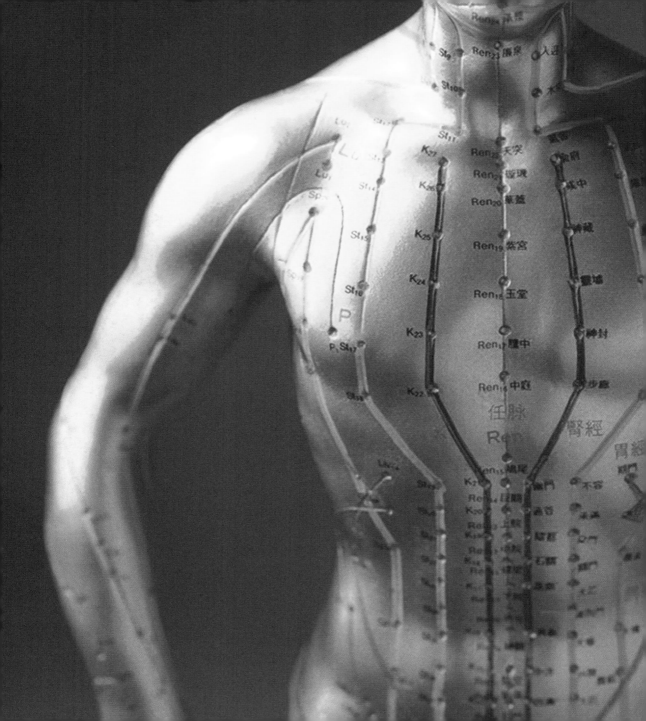

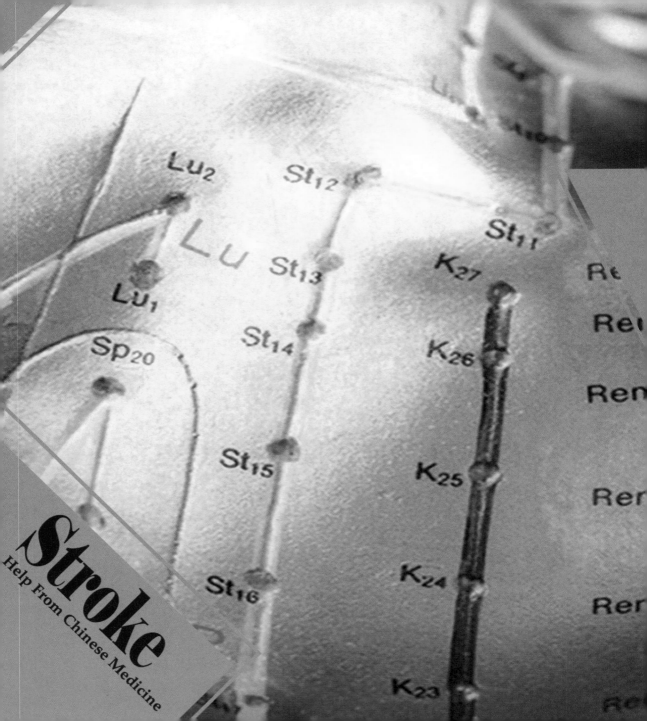

Lu₂ St₁₂

Lu

St₁₁

St₁₃

K₂₇ Re

Lu₁

K₂₆ Ren

St₁₄

SP₂₀

K₂₅ Ren

St₁₅

K₂₄ Ren

St₁₆

K₂₃ Re

Stroke
Help From Chinese Medicine

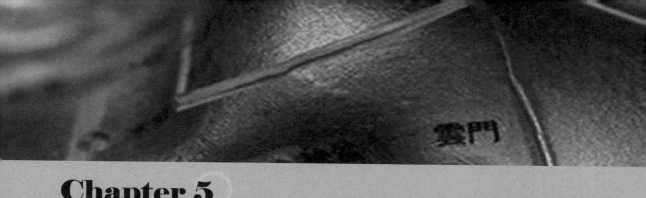

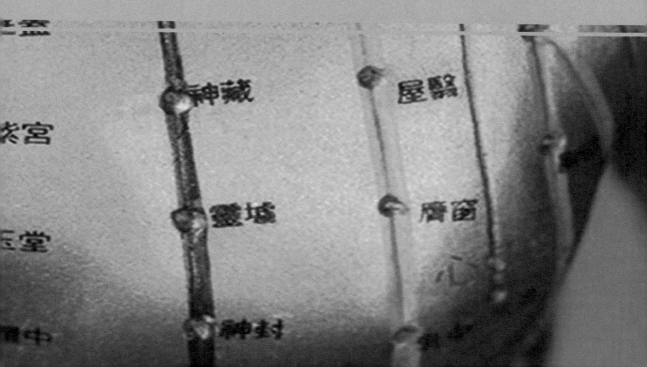

Case Studies

This last chapter offers some case studies, where combined treatments have been used to cure stroke. The concept and details of treating with TCM can be learned from these cases. They also serve as evidence that patients can be cured by the methods mentioned already.

Case

Female, 56 years old.

First visit: Dec 22, 2008

Chief Complaint: right side paralysis for more than 7 months.

History of present illness: 7 months ago, the patient had a headache and dizziness, but she ignored it. A few days later she had a stroke which caused right side paralysis. After the hemiparalysis, she was given many drugs and physiotherapy, but they were not effective. She came to the TCM hospital expecting to receive systematic treatment. Present indications: Right side paralysis, the left side normal, fluent speech, normal appetite, stomach ache, chronic constipation once in 5 days, no food preferences, and CT examination showing cerebral infarction.

History of past illness: hypertension for 2 years; highest blood pressure reading is 170/110mmHg, and is not on regular medication. Hyperlipidemia; details of the disease is unknown.

Physical examination: clear consciousness, low spirits, light tenderness on right upper quadrant. Muscle strength of right upper and lower limbs grade 0, the left normal, the forehead striation existed. Pathological reflex of right body positive. Pink tongue with white coat, and a deep, internal pulse.

Diagnosis: stoke-apoplexy involving both collaterals and channels.

Pattern identification: qi stagnation and blood stasis, channels lacking nourishment.

Therapeutic principles: supplement qi and activate blood circulation, relax tendons and activate collaterals.

Prescription: modified *Bù Yáng Huán Wǔ Tāng*

Herbs	Pinyin	Dose	Latin Name
黄芪	*huáng qí*	20 g	Radix Astragali
当归	*dāng guī*	10 g	Radix Angelicae Sinensis
赤芍	*chì sháo*	10 g	Radix Paeoniae Rubra
川芎	*chuān xiōng*	10 g	Rhizoma Chuanxiong
地龙	*dì lóng*	10 g	Pheretima
丹参	*dān shēn*	10 g	Radix et Rhizoma Salviae Miltiorrhizae
姜黄	*jiāng huáng*	10 g	Rhizoma Curcumae Longae
桑枝	*sāng zhī*	10 g	Ramulus Mori
伸筋草	*shēn jīn cǎo*	10 g	Herba Lycopodii
忍冬藤	*rěn dōng téng*	15 g	Caulis Lonicerae Japonicae
苏梗	*sū gěng*	10 g	Caulis Perillae
大黄	*dài huáng*	9 g	Radix et Rhizoma Rhei

Chinese patent medicine: *Xiang Sha Liu Jun* pills, 2 boxes, 6 g twice a day

Acupuncture points: LI 4, PC 6, LI 11, LI 10, LI 15 (*Jiān Yú*) 肩髃, GB 30, DU 14 (*dà zhuī*) 大椎, SP10, ST36, GB34, and SP6.

Medical order: regularly use decompression treatment; take aspirin 75 mg daily; begin rehabilitation exercise as soon as possible.

Second visit: Dec 29, 2009

After taking the herbal decoctions, most of her symptoms were alleviated; palpitations occurred occasionally but not as frequently as before, appetite was low and stools occurred once every four days; these were the only symptoms the patient reported. Tongue and pulse presentations were same as before. The herbal decoction was made up on the basis of the first visit, with a few changes: tumeric root was removed, the dosage of rhubarb was doubled, and dried rehmannia root was added. Other treatments were the same as the first visit.

Herbs	Pinyin	Dose	Latin Name
黄芪	*huáng qí*	20 g	Radix Astragali
当归	*dāng guī*	10 g	Radix Angelicae Sinensis
赤芍	*chì sháo*	10 g	Radix Paeoniae Rubra
川芎	*chuān xiōng*	10 g	Rhizoma Chuanxion
地龙	*dì lóng*	10 g	Pheretima
丹参	*dān shēn*	10 g	Radix et Rhizoma Salviae Miltiorrhizae
桑枝	*sāng zhī*	10 g	Ramulus Mori
伸筋草	*shēn jīn cǎo*	10 g	Herba Lycopodii
忍冬藤	*rěn dōng téng*	15 g	Caulis Lonicerae Japonicae
苏梗	*sū gěng*	10 g	Caulis Perillae
大黄	*dà huáng*	9 g	Radix et Rhizoma Rhei
生地	*shēng dì*	15 g	Radix Rehmanniae

Third visit: Jan 7, 2010

After taking the second herbal decoction, almost all of the symptoms were alleviated; palpitations stopped, appetite increased, stools were once every two days, and the patient had no other discomfort. Muscle strength on the right side was grade 1. The prescription remained the same as the second visit; no changes were implemented.

Discussion: there is a definite diagnosis in this case; the patient had hypertensive disease and hyperlipidemia, but she ignored these health conditions, which led to cerebral thrombosis forming. We can learn from this case that prevention and medical education is very important for patients. They should be aware of how to create a healthy life, and make sure they maintain it. The pattern identification of the case study above is qi stagnation and blood stasis, which is the classical pattern of stroke in TCM. Using treatment of classical herbal decoctions of Bu Yang Huan Wu Tang to increase vital energy and activate blood circulation, the results were very effective. It is also very important to maintain regular bowel movements in stroke patients, as this is beneficial to their recovery.

Conclusion

The prevention and treatment of stroke is a long-term process, that requires patience and confidence of both doctor and patient. In the acute phase of stroke, especially when patients lose consciousness, we recommend that they are immediately sent to hospital for treatment. Whilst being treated with western medicine, traditional Chinese medicine therapies can simultaneously be utilized to ensure a more effective, and faster recovery, while also reducing side effects. As you have seen from the previous information, there are many methods in which to treat stroke using Chinese medicine, and all of them are effective to an extent. The key is to identify the correct pattern, which is of utmost importance to then determine correct and effective treatment. With precise pattern identification, half the work will get double the results from herbal and acupuncture therapy. Although the therapies

of Chinese medicine are generally safe, the help of a qualified practitioner is necessary for diagnosis and the administration of some methods. However there are some techniques and tips which are simple enough to be followed on your own.

Here we summarize the treatments of stroke mentioned previously, and offer some suggestions:

In the prevention of disease, TCM emphasizes "prevent disease before it arises" and "prevent disease from developing". Experts suggest that the comprehensive approaches, including medicinal treatment, lifestyle, diet, climate changes and the healthcare of mental activities, should be considered for the prevention of stroke. If necessary, a combined treatment of traditional Chinese medicine and western medicine can be used[83].

The method of activating blood and resolving obstruction is one of the most effective methods for the treatment of stroke; this is indicated in the acute stage, convalescence stage, and the sequela stage of stroke[84,85].

On the basis of patient observation, we can select the formulas and medicinals dynamically, and change them according to the change of patterns, at different periods. Integrated use of Chinese medicinal injections, oral decoctions of Chinese medicinals, acupuncture and moxibustion, rehabilitation, foot soaks, and other measures on the basis of internal medicine therapy are the major treatment modalities for stroke[86,87].

Bǔ Yáng Huán Wǔ Tāng (Yang-Supple-Menting Five-Returning Decoction) and the Chinese patent medicines which have the function of tonifying qi and activating blood, are indicated for the treatment of qi deficiency and blood obstruction pattern of stroke. There is much ancient and modern literature on *Bǔ Yáng Huán Wǔ Tāng* (Yang-Supplementing Five-Returning Decoction) for the treatment of stroke, mostly for convalescence and sequela stages. The patients in acute stage can also be treated with it on the basis of clinical pattern identification. Years of clinical practice and scientific research shows that *Bǔ Yáng Huán Wǔ Tāng* (Yang-Supplementing Five-Returning Decoction) is an effective formula for the treatment of stroke, and has been widely accepted in the western and Chinese medical fields, and has become one of the most widely used formulas in the treatment of stroke currently[88].

After the stroke attacks, about 40%-50% of acute stroke patients show a pattern of excess phlegm heat in the bowels, and the key points of treatment should focus on transforming phlegm and freeing the bowels, to restore the functions of the bowels and viscera, the channels, qi and blood.

In the treatment of patients with visceral and bowel stroke in wind-stroke, the method of opening up the orifices can be used. An Gong Niu Huang Wan (Peaceful Palace Bovine Bezoar Pill), Zhi Bao Dan (Supreme Jewel Elixir) or Su He Xiang Wan (Storax Pill) should be selected according to clinical pattern identification.

The methods of treating complications after stroke with TCM mainly include acupuncture and moxibustion, Chinese medicinal bathing, tui na and massage. The combined treatments with current western rehabilitation medicine, can enhance the recovery[89].

In the field of TCM, systematic research has been conducted on the prevention, treatment, and rehabilitation of stroke. As a result, a consensus has been reached on the therapeutic mode and approach for treating cerebral apoplexy with TCM. The treatment plans for stroke have been progressively studied and high level efficacy found in evidence based medicine (EBM).

Treating stroke with TCM emphasizes the principle of pattern identification and treatment i.e., treating patients according to the changes of patterns at different stages of stroke. At the acute stage, the commonly used treatment methods are opening the orifices, resolving phlegm to unblock bowels and collaterals, and smoothing the liver to extinguish wind. At the convalescence and sequelae stages, the commonly used treatment methods are tonifying qi and activating blood, enrich-

ing yin and unblocking collaterals. The therapies include Chinese medicinal decoctions (taken orally or by nasal feeding), Chinese patent medicine, acupuncture and moxibustion, tui na, foot soaks, and rehabilitation training.

The above methods should be selected based on the clinical characteristics at different stages and patients' conditions. It is preferable to use comprehensive methods, which can promote the recovery of the nerve function and improve the quality of patients' lives.

Appendix

1. The Assessment of Activities in the Recovery from Stroke

The assessment of activity limitation (disability) level, which refers to the assessment of individual disability level and dysfunction, is generally evaluated by observing the Activities of Daily Living (ADL). Because "activities of daily living" is essential for everyone, the basic purpose of rehabilitation is to improve the patient's activities of daily living. This is not only the basis upon which the rehabilitation goals, plans and assessments are built, but also a very important step in the recovery treatment.

The Basic of Physical ADL (BADL or PADL) refers to the basic human activities such as sitting, standing, walking, and self care activities such as dressing, feeding, personal hygiene, and others. Amongst all the standardized evaluation methods of PADL, Barthel index is the most widely used.

The Barthel index of ADL consists of 10 parts: eating, bathing, grooming, dressing, bowel control, urinary control, using the toilet, bed chair transfer, walking on ground, and walking up and down stairs. It is rated on 4 levels: 15, 10, 5 and 0, according to whether the patient needs help, and how much is required. The index sums up scores of all parts. 100 for those who are completely competent, which shows that the patient functions well in daily life and does not require any help. 0 indicates the patient cannot live by himself, which means all the basic activities must be carried out by other people. The details and evaluating standards are listed below.

The Barthel Index (BADL) ♋

Activity
FEEDING
0 = unable
5 = needs help cutting, spreading butter, etc., or requires modified diet
10 = independent
BATHING
0 = dependent on others
5 = independent (or in shower)
GROOMING
0 = needs help with personal care
5 = independent care of face/hair/teeth/shaving (implements provided)
DRESSING
0 = dependent on others

5 = needs help, but can do some un-aided

10 = independent (including buttons, zips, laces, etc.)

BOWELS

0 = incontinent (or needs to be given enemas)

5 = occasional accident

10 = continent

BLADDER

0 = incontinent, or catheterized and unable to manage alone

5 = occasional accident

10 = continent

TOILET USE

0 = dependent on others

5 = needs some help, but can do something alone

10 = independent (on and off, dressing, wiping)

TRANSFERS (BED TO CHAIR AND BACK)

0 = unable, no sitting balance

5 = major help (one or two people for physical assistance), can sit

10 = minor help (verbal or physical assistance)

15 = independent

MOBILITY (ON LEVEL SURFACES)

0 = immobile or < 50 yards

5 = wheelchair independent, including corners, > 50 yards

10 = walks with help of one person (verbal or physical assistance) > 50 yards

15 = independent (but may use any aid; for example, stick) > 50 yards

STAIRS

0 = unable

5 = needs help (verbal, physical, carrying aid)

10 = independent

TOTAL (0–100):

The barthel ADL index: guidelines ⟨ʔ

➤ The index should be used as a record of what a patient does, not as a record of what a patient could do.

➤ The main aim is to establish a degree of independence from any help, physical or verbal, however minor and for whatever reason.

➤ The need for supervision renders the patient not independent.

➤ A patient's performance should be established using the best available evidence. Asking the patient, friends/relatives and nurses are the usual sources, but direct observation and common sense are also important. However direct testing is not required.

➤ Usually the patient's performance over the preceding 24-48 hours is important, but occasionally longer periods will be relevant.

➤ Middle categories imply that the patient supplies over 50% of the effort.

➤ Use of aids to be independent is allowed.

The ADL is rated on 3 levels: good, moderate and poor, according to the Barthel Index.

➤ >60 is good, mild dysfunction; able to complete part of their daily activities, need some help

➤ 60-41 is moderate, with moderate dysfunction; requires a tremendous amount of help to complete activities in daily living

➤ ≤40 is poor, with severe dysfunction; most of the activities of daily living cannot be performed or require others to serve

Barthel Index is comprehensive, easy to use, reliable and sensitive. It can also be used to predict the effect of treatment, length of stay in hospital, and prognosis. Clinical studies have shown that among patients who are hospitalized within 1 month, and rated on the Barthel Index, of those rated between 0 and 20, 35% would be dead, 16% could return home; among those who were rated between 60-100, 95% could return home. Treatment for 2-3 months would raise the index to 30. Patients who rated between 40-60 recovered the best.

2. Basic Disease Information

Some factors that lead to stroke are already known and can be prevented, including hypertension, smoking, obesity, increased serum fibrinogen levels, diabetes, lack of exercise, and birth control with high dosage estrogen. The most critical factor, and also the easiest to deal with, is systolic hypertension. In a program studying multiple factors, it is shown that 40% of strokes were led by high blood pressure over 140 mmHg. The incidence of stroke also increases exponentially when the patients' age increases. The incidence is 3/100,000 among people between 30-40 years old, and raised to 300/100,000 among those who are between 80-90 years old. 88% of stroke fatalities are those over 65 years old. The table below showed controllable and uncontrollable factors.

Risk factors

Factors of dangerous		Relative risk (per 1,000 person)
Controllable	High blood pressure	4.0~5.0
	Cardiac disease	2.0~4.0
	AFIB	5.6~17.6
	Diabetes	1.5~3.0
	Smoking	1.5~2.9
	Alcohol abuse	1.0~4.0
	Hyperlipidemia	1.0~2.0
Uncontrollable	Age	1~2/1000 (between the age of 45 and 54)
		20/1000 (between the age of 75 and 84)
	Race	1.2~2.1
	Genetics	2.0

Methods to promote stroke management ⏲

The prevention of stroke is mainly through controlling high blood pressure in the elderly. Another reason for the decrease in mortality has been through the establishment of the Stroke Unit, which reduces mortality in the acute phase, and prevents further harmful complications.

The stroke unit usually works as a team.

The stroke unit team consists of:

➢ Rehabilitation physicians: responsible for patient admissions, collecting history, and developing rehabilitation plans

➢ TCM doctors: responsible for providing TCM treatments and health advice to patients

➢ Acupuncture and massage, MD: providing acupuncture or massage therapy to relieve pain, and promoting the recovery of movement and perception functions

➢ Physiotherapist: providing physical treatment

➢ Occupational therapist: guiding patients to perform daily living training

➢ Speech therapist: providing training and rehabilitation education for patients who have speech impairment, or swallowing dysfunction

➢ Rehabilitation nurse: providing general clinical care and rehabilitation care

➢ Psychotherapist: providing psychological counseling and psychotherapy, and improving patients' motivation

➢ Music therapist: regulating patients' emotions, and improving motor coordination

3. Additional Reading Material

Chinese Medicine ♫

➢ Xu Yi-bing. *An Illustrated Guide to Chinese Medicine*. People's Medical Publishing House, 2007

➢ Paul Pitchford. *Healing With Whole Foods: Asian Traditions and Modern Nutrition*. North Atlantic Books, 2003

➢ Harriet Beinfield, Efrem Korngold. *Between Heaven and Earth. Random* House, 1991

➢ Tom Williams. *Complete Illustrated Guide to Chinese Medicine*. Barnes & Noble INC, 1996

➢ Yang Jia-san. *The Way to Locate Acupoints*. Foreign Language Press, 1982

➢ Li De-yin. *Tai ji Quan*. Foreign Language Press, 2004

➢ Cai Jing-feng. *Eating Your Way to Health*

– *Diet Therapy in Traditional Chinese Medicine*. Foreign Language Press, 1996

➢ http://www.acupuncture.com/education/tcmbasics/index.htm
➢ http://www.acupuncturetoday.com/abc/
➢ http://www.healthy.net/
➢ http://nccam.nih.gov/health/
➢ http://www.tcmstudent.com/
➢ http://www.nlm.nih.gov/hmd/chinese/chinesehome.html
➢ http://qi-journal.com/
➢ http://www.medicalacupuncture.org/
➢ http://nccam.nih.gov/
➢ http://www.herbnet.com/
➢ http://www.medical-acupuncture.co.uk/
➢ http://www.acupuncture.com/referrals/can.htm

Stroke Management ♫

➢ Pan Chang. *Rehabilitation of paralysis due to apoplexy*. Foreign Language Press, 2004

➢ Medicine Research Institute. *Acupuncture Research*. People's Health Press, 1981:318 - 319

➢ Wang Jian-zhong. *Acupuncture and rehabilitation of stroke in modern*. Science and Technology Literature Publishing House, 2007.7

➢ He Guang-xin. *Rehabilitation and acupuncture of stroke*. Chinese Medicine Press, 1997.11

4. How to Find a Practitioner of Chinese Medicine

Finding a practitioner of Chinese medicine is often as easy as looking in your local phone book. Most cities now have an "Acupuncture" heading in the yellow pages. Since acupuncture is the most well known modality of Chinese medicine in western countries, those that practice Chinese herbalism will often also be listed in this section. In many places, there will probably not be a practitioner who specializes in treating stroke but you may be able to find someone in the larger cities if you call around.

Most countries have established educational and licensure standards. A practitioner should be able to verify that these standards have been met.

The web can offer many ways to find a practitioner. Just searching for "acupuncture" and your town/area's name will probably locate something. The following internet resources should help you find a practitioner in your local area:

International Acupuncture Referral	http://www.acufinder.com http://www.gancao.net
Australia	Australian Acupuncture and Chinese Medicine Association http://www.acupuncture.org.au/
Canada	Traditional Chinese Medicine Association of British Columbia http://tcmabc.org/ Ordre des Acupuncteurs, Quebec http://www.ordredesacupuncteurs.qc.ca/
New Zealand	New Zealand Registrar of Acupuncture http://acupuncture.org.nz/
United Kingdom	Register of Chinese Herbal Medicine http://www.rchm.cwww.acupuncture.org.uk/ The British Medical Acupuncture Society http://www.medical-acupuncture.co.uk/
United States of America	National Certification Commission for Acupuncture and Oriental Medicine http://nccaom.org/ Council of Colleges of Acupuncture and Oriental Medicine http://www.ccaom.org/
Tai Ji - Qi Gong Information	http://www.worldtaichiday.org http://www.qi.org

Reference

1. Adams H. P. Jr, Del Zoppo G., Alberts M. J., Bhatt D. L., Brass L., Furlan A., Grubb R. L., Higashida R. T., Jauch E. C., Kidwell C., Lyden P. D., Morgenstern L. B., Qureshi A. I., Rosenwasser R. H., Scott P. A., Wijdicks E. F. M., American Heart Association, American Stroke Association Stroke Council, Clinical Cardiology Council. Guidelines for the early management of adults with ischemic stroke: a guideline from the American Heart Association/American Stroke Association Stroke Council, Clinical Cardiology Council, Cardiovascular Radiology [trunc]. *Stroke*. 2007 38(5): 1655-711.

2. Goldstein L. B., Adams R., Alberts M. J., Appel L. J., Brass L. M., Bushnell C. D., Culebras A., DeGraba T. J., Gorelick P. B., Guyton J. R., Hart R. G., Howard G., Kelly-Hayes M., Nixon J. V., Sacco R. L., American Heart Association, American Stroke Association Stroke Council. Primary prevention of ischemic stroke: a guideline from the American Heart Association/American Stroke Association Stroke Council [trunc]. *Circulation*. 2006,113(24): e873-923.

3. ZhongHai-zhen. Preliminary Study on Cause of Disability in Patients with Ischemic Apoplexy *Chinese Journal of Basic Medicine in Traditional Chinese Medicine*. 2010, 16(1): 47-49.

4. Gao Ying, Dan Shen. Elation between Phlegm Syndrome of Ischemic Stroke and C Reactive Protein and Neurological Impairment. *Liaoning Journal of Traditional Chinese Medicine*. 37(3): 429-430.

5. Sacco R. L., Adams R., Albers G., Alberts M. J., Benavente O., Furie K., Goldstein L. B., Gorelick P., Halperin J., Harbaugh R., Johnston S. C., Katzan I., Kelly-Hayes M., Kenton E. J., Marks M., Schwamm L. H., Tomsick T.. Guidelines for prevention of stroke in patients with ischemic stroke or transient ischemic attack: a statement for healthcare professionals from the American Heart Association/American Stroke Association Council on Stroke [trunc]. *Stroke*. 2006,37(2): 577-617.

6. Singapore Ministry of Health. Stroke and transient ischemic attacks:

assessment, investigation, immediate management and secondary prevention. Singapore: Singapore Ministry of Health. 2003 Mar.

7. Tao Ye, Zhang Yun-ling. Study on the relationship between fire-blood stasis syndrome and coagulation factors in patients with acute ischemic stroke. *China Journal of Traditional Chinese Medicine and Pharmacy*. 2010,4(12): 367-368.

8. Zhang Guo-ping, Xue Ping. Extracranial carotid occlusive lesions in aged patients with cerebral infarction (a report of 100 cases). *China Journal of Modern Medicine*. 2010,20(8): 1262-1264.

9. Wang You-qi, Li Kai, Wang Lu. Mechanisms of "Qingnao Suppository" in Acting on Acute Cerebral Edema, Neuron Injury, and Neuropeptide in Focal Ischemic Rats. *Shanghai Journal of Traditional Chinese Medicine*. 2008,42 (7): 81-83.

10. Zhou Zhong-ying. Views on the Method of Cooling Blood and Removing Blood Stasis in Treating Hemorrhagic and Ischemic Stroke. *Journal of Nanjing University of Traditional Chinese Medicine*. 1999,22(1): 61-63.

11. Zhao Z, Xie Y, Meng F, et al. Dynamic Analysis of TCM Syndrome Elements Based on the Neuropsychological Characteristics of Cognitive Function Impairment after Ischemic Stroke. *Journal of Traditional Chinese Medicine*. 2010, 51(3): 256-258.

12. Xu J., Gao Y., Wang Z.. Study on the Relationship between the TCM Syndromes and Neurological Impairment of Stroke. *Journal of Traditional Chinese Medicine*. 2010,51(6): 540-542.

13. Wu Yun, Sun Xing-hua, Xing Yue. Intervening Effect of Point-to-point Acupuncture on Post-stroke Depression and its Influence on Plasma Hydrocortisone Levels. *Shanghai Journal of Acupuncture and Moxibustion*. 2006,27(7): 804-807.

14. Pan Sheng-lian. Research Advances of Integrated of Traditional Chinese Medicine and Western Medicine in Treating Post-stroke Depression. *Journal of Liaoning University of Traditional Chinese Medicine*. 2002,29(6): 331-332.

15. Institute for Clinical Systems Improvement (ICSI). Diagnosis and initial treatment of ischemic stroke. Bloomington (MN): Institute for Clinical Systems Improvement (ICSI). 2006 Feb.

16. New Zealand Guidelines Group (NZGG). Life after stroke. New Zealand guidelines for management of stroke. Wellington (NZ): New Zealand Guidelines

Group (NZGG). 2003 Nov.

17. Yukito Shinohara, Takashi Yoshimoto, YasuoFukuuchi, ShigenobuIshigami. The Joint Committee on Guidelines for the Management of Stroke. Japanese Guidelines for the Management of Stroke. 2004. Kyowa Kikaku, Ltd. Tokyo, 2004.

18. Wang Ying, Zhao Hai,et al. Reliability, Validity and Response of Patient-Reported-Outcome Scale in Stroke Patients with Spastic Paralysis. *Chinese General Practice*. 2009,12(7): 1168-1170.

19. Chen Bao-xin, Zhang Yun-ling. Correlation between stroke syndrome factors and neurological impairment scores. *Journal of Beijing University of Traditional Chinese Medicine*. 2004;328: 1490-1497.

20. Zhang Yan-hong, Liu Bao-yan, et al. Analysis on Reliability and Validity of the Evaluation Scale of Patient-Reported-Outcome Based on the Windstroke Patients with Spastic Paralysis. *Journal of Traditional Chinese Medicine*. 2008,49(8): 698-700.

21. Huang Yu-yu. Observations on the Efficacy of Acupuncture plus Rehabilitation in Treating Stroke Hemiplegia. *Shanghai Journal of Acupuncture and Moxibustion*. 2010,3(7): 59-61.

22. National Institute for Health and Clinical Excellence (NICE). Alteplase for the treatment of acute ischemic stroke. London (UK): *National Institute for Health and Clinical Excellence*. 2007 ,22 (7): 231.

23. Hu Xuan-zhou, Li Guo-an, Wang Bo. Advances in Studies of Acupuncture-moxibustion Treatment andMassotherapyfor Post-stroke Hypermyotonia. *Shanghai Journal of Acupuncture and Moxibustion*. 2009,7(12): 49-50.

24. Wan Jiao, Li Bo, Chen Xiang-yang. Observations on the Efficacy of Contralateral Meridian Needling-induced Complex Acupuncture in Restoring the Motor Function of Hemiplegic Stroke Patients. *Shanghai Journal of Acupuncture and Moxibustion*. 2006,22(2): 3-35.

25. Sha Kai-hui,LiuKui-kui. Investigation of the effect of Taijiquan exercise on the heartof the elderly. *Liaoning Journal of Traditional Chinese Medicine*. 2010,37(6): 975-978.

26. Li Xing-hai. Effect of Qigong? Baduanjin on Endothelium-dependent Arterial Dilation of Type 2 Diabetes. *Journal of Shenyang Sport University*. 2009,28(1): 610.

27. Mao Yan. The influences of Taijiquan and comprehensive exercises on

blood lipid metabolism of senile women. *Chinese Journal of Woman and Child Health Research*. 2007,26(7): 176-177.

28. WangFang,Wang Wei-dong . Influences of different qigong practices on sleep quality in patients with type 2 diabetes accompanied by insomnia. *Journal of Beijing University of Traditional Chinese Medicine*. 2009,9(12): 312.

29. Wang Ze-ying,Zhao Man-li. Effect of Health Education in Stroke Unit of Medicine on Stroke with Qi Deficiency. *Chinese Journal of Interative medicine on Cardio-Cerebrovascular Disease*. 2007, 5(3): 563-564.

30. Ran Bin. Different Exercise Intensities on Cardiovascular Function in the Elderly Impact Analysis. *Chinese Journal of Basic Medicine in Traditional Chinese Medicine*. 2010,16(4): 325-327. *Chinese Manipulation & Qi Gong Therapy*. 2008,8(5): 127-128.

31. Liu Shan-yun. The Intervention of Taijiquan on Blood Lipids and Ig of Abnormal Blood Lipids Patient. *Journal of Traditional Chinese Medicine*. 2006,47(12): 920-921.

32. Li Chan-wu,ZengY. Effect of Taijiquan on endothelial diastolic function in the elderly. *Journal of Traditional Chinese Medicine*. 2006,47(5): 378-380.

33. Li Zhao-wei,Zhou Li-juan. Observation on Patients with Dyslipidemia Treated by Five -animal Exercises. *Journal of Guangzhou Physical Education Institute*. 2009,29(4): 669.

34. Brosseau L., Wells G. A., Finestone H. M., Egan M., Dubouloz C. J., Graham I., Casimiro L., Robinson V. A., Bilodeau M., McGowan J.. Clinical practice guidelines for acupuncture. Top Stroke Rehabilitation. 2006 Spring;13(2): 657.

35. Liu Jian-hao. Observation on specificity of acupuncture location in treatment of acute apoplexy by scalp penetration needling. *Chinese Acupuncture & Moxibustion*, 2010,30(4) : 275-276.

36. JiXue-qun. Observation on therapeutic effect of nuchal acupuncture and abdominal acupuncture for treatment of stroke patients with spastic hemiplegia. *Chinese Acupuncture & Moxibustion*. 2009, 29(12): 961-964.

37. Sällström S, Kjendahl A, Osten P. E. Acupuncture therapy in stroke during the subacute phase. *Tidsskr Nor Laegeforen*. 1995,115(23): 2884-7.

38. Jin Ze, Li Zhao-xian. Clinical Observations on Double-needle Acupuncture for the Treatment of Post-stroke Leg Hy-

permyotonia. *Shanghai Journal of Acupuncture and Moxibustion.* 2007,32(7): 397-398.

39. Frank Kai-hoi Sze, Eric Wong, Kevin K. H.. Does Acupuncture Improve Motor Recovery After Stroke? A Meta-Analysis of Randomized Controlled Trials. *Stroke,* 2002,33: 2604.

40. Wang Hai-qiao, Chen Ming, Liu Jian-hao. Clinical Research Survey on Methods of Scalp Acupuncture Treatment for Apoplectic Hemiplegia. *Journal of Liaoning University of Traditional Chinese Medicine.* 2006,10(43): 37.

41. Liu Zhi-shun, Wang Li-ping, Yang Guang, et al. Effect of the Acupuncture Method "Regulating the Sea of Marrow, Circulating Yang and Soothing Tendons" on Quality of Life and Activity of Daily Living in Hemiplegia Patients. *Journal of Traditional Chinese Medicine.* 2008,49(2): 138-141.

42. Wu Heng, Tang xin. *Acupuncture for stroke rehabilitation.* Cochrane Database Syst Rev. 2006,19: 4131.

43. Shen Qing, QiuJia. Clinical Study on Treating Post-stroke Depression By Head Matrix Acupuncture. *Liaoning Journal of Traditional Chinese Medicine.* 2010,37(4): 718-720.

44. ZengXue-qing. Observations on the Efficacy of Acupuncture as Main Treatment for Post-stroke Dysphagia. *Shanghai Journal of Acupuncture and Moxibustion.* 2000,17(1): 9-14.

45. Meng Xiang-dong. Clinical Observations on the Efficacy of Auricular Point Plaster Therapy plus Acupuncture, in Treating Post-stroke Depression of Liver-Kidney Yin Deficiency Type. *Shanghai Journal of Acupuncture and Moxibustion.* 2003,21(7): 291-292.

46. Pin Wang, Yang Hua-yan. Impedance characteristics of ear acupoints in identifying excess or deficiency syndrome of stroke. *Journal of Chinese Integrative Medicine.* 2000,23(4): 4-6.

47. Hang Wei, Wang Jian. Joint treatment of apoplexy sequela by tongue acupuncture and head acupuncture. *Information on Traditional Chinese Medicine.* 2006,26(2): 141-146.

48. Jin Ze, Wang Lin-jing. Clinical Observations on Acupuncture at Huatuojiaji Points for the Treatment of Post-stroke Hemiplegic Spasticity. *Shanghai Journal of Acupuncture and Moxibustion.* 2002,23(3): 56-57.

49. Shen Wei-na. Clinical Observations on Yin-reducing Acupuncture for the

Treatment of Post-stroke Spastic Hemiplegia. *Shanghai Journal of Acupuncture and Moxibustion*. 2005,5(2): 101-105.

50. Zhao Ying-ding. Observations on the Therapeutic Effect of Acupuncture plus Rehabilitation on Hemiplegic Stroke. *Shanghai Journal of Acupuncture and Moxibustion*. 1999, 16(4); 263-267.

51. PengHui-yuan, He Xi-jun. Effect of Electroacupuncture at Temporal Three Needle Acupoints as Main Treatment on Activities of Daily Living and Quality of Life in Patients with Post-stroke Depression. *Shanghai Journal of Acupuncture and Moxibustion*. 2004,27(3): 21-24.

52. Ni Huan-huan, Cui Xiao. Clinical Observations on the Efficacy of Superficial Needling plus Functional Training in Treating Shoulder-hand Syndrome. *Shanghai Journal of Acupuncture and Moxibustion*. 2003, 18(4): 494-495.

53. Chen Yun-li. AcupunctureTreat Post-stroke Shoulder-hand Syndrome. *Journal of Zhejiang University of Traditional Chinese Medicine*. 2007,2(2): 76-78.

54. Mei Lin-feng; Fang Xiang-dong. Clinical observation on the efficacy of coma patients resulting from cerebral hemorrhage treated with scalp,ear and body acupuncture combined with "sharpening mind and inducing consciousness" acupuncture method. *Modern Medicine & Health*. 2008,24(7): 1312-1313.

55. Liu Hai-tao,Zhu Wen-hong. Effect of auricular plaster and Erjian bleedingon blood lipid in patients with hyperlipoproteinemia. *Journal of TCM University of Hunan*. 2009,29(3): 978-979.

56. Lv Hang-zhou,Wang Qing-chun. Study on the intervention effect of auricular acupuncture on hippocampus neuronal apoptosis in rats with vasculardementia. *Chinese Journal of Gerontology*. 2009,31(14): 561-562.

57. Hu Jing-jing ,Liu Yue-cai. Therapeutic effects of scalp-acupuncture in patients with vascular dementia induced by cerebral infarction: a randomized controlled trial. *ActaUniversitatis Traditions MedicalisSinensisPharmacologiaeque Shanghai*. 2008; 6(8): 806-809.

58. CaiHeng. Observation on clinical therapeutic effect of scalp acupuncture combined with body acupuncture on apoplectic hemiplegia. *Chinese Acupuncture &Moxibustion*. 2006, 26(6): 1021-1022.

59. LI Xiao-jun,LiuWen-dan,HUCaihong. Influence of Concomitant Scalp Acupuncture and Kinetotherapy on Somatosensory Evoked Potential in Hemi-

plegia Patients. *Shanghai Journal of Acupuncture and Moxibustion*. 2009,28(10): 867.

60. Wang Dao-hai,SunHua ,et al. Effect of Acupuncture on Different Traditional Chinese Medicine Syndrome Types in Patients with Apoplectic Hemiplegia. *Journal of Beijing University of Traditional Chinese Medicine*. 2007,21(8): 262-263.

61. Li Xiao-jun,ZhengBin. Observations on the Efficacy of Early Scalp Acupuncture plus Modern Rehabilitation Techniques in Treating Postapoplectic Hemiplegia. *Shanghai Journal of Acupuncture and Moxibustion*. 2009,28(7): 438-439.

62. Wang Li-na. A fMRI Study of the Effects of Acupuncture on Cerebral Function Activities of Subjects with Ischemic Apoplexy during Index Finger Movement. *Shanghai Journal of Acupuncture and Moxibustion*. 2004,21(3): 215-219.

63. Wang Jian-wei, Yang Ning. Comprehensive therapy for elderly patients with stroke. *Journal of Traditional Chinese Medicine University of Hunan*. 2003,1(9): 512-514.

64. Xin Xi-yan, Zhang Hua. Relationship between TCM prescriptions and syndrome elements in acute ischemic stroke. *China Journal of Traditional Chinese Medicine and Pharmacy*. 2004,9(9): 1023-1025 .

65. Li Xia,Yu Xia. Analysis of The Relationship Between Chinese Medicine Dialectical Type and TCD Diagnosis to Stroke. *Chinese Archives of Traditional Chinese Medicine*. 2005,5(7): 549-555.

66. Hong Li-fen, Guo Hong-min. Application Research of Bu Yang Huan Wu Tangin Heart and Cerebrovascular Disease. *Journal of Liaoning University of Traditional Chinese Medicine*. 2003,1(8): 493-494.

67. Xiang Yun, Tu Qin, Xiao Qiu. Clinical effect of Honghuahuangsesu injection on ischemic apoplexy. *Chinese Journal of Hospital Pharmacy*. 2008,28(7): 1493-1495.

68. Cheng Fa-feng, Wang Qing-guo. Therapy of clearing heat, removing toxins and activating blood circulation is important to ischemic stroke in acute stage. *Journal of Beijing University of Traditional Chinese Medicine*. 2005,4(2): 55-57.

69. Wang Ying-ying, Yang Jin-sheng. Analysis on symptoms of 216 patients with heat-phlegm and sthenic-fusyndrome in the acute stage of apoplexy. *Journal of Beijing University of Traditional Chinese Medicine*. 2008,31(5): 347-350.

70. Wang Yan-hua. 58 clinical observation cases of comprehensive TCM treatment in early Ischemic Stroke. *Chinese Archives of Traditional Chinese Medicine*.

2007,24(2): 168-173.

71. Zhang Hong-xin. Chinese Medicine in Hemorrhagic Stroke Treatment during recent Years. *Journal of Liaoning University of Traditional Chinese Medicine.* 1998,21(4): 44-50.

72. Wang Li-xin, Cai Ye-feng, Guo-Jian-wen. Effect of Integrative Medical Therapy on the Prognosis of Patients Suffering from Yin Syndrome Type Acute Ischemic Stroke. *Chinese Journal of Integrated Traditional and Western Medicine.* 2009,22(7): 129-130.

73. Zhang Qiu-xia,ZhaoHui. Discussion of Wind-drug Acting as Medicinal Guide. *Journal of Liaoning University of Traditional Chinese Medicine.* 2001,19(9): 29.

74. ZhongXue-wen, Zou Yi-hua. Changes of TCM symptoms in acute stroke seizure phase, and correlation between symptoms and matrix metalloproteinase-9. *China Journal of Traditional Chinese Medicine and Pharmacy.* 2006,17(10): 432-435.

75. Xie Yan-ming, Yu Wen-ya. Study on Therapeutic Window of TCM Synthesis Project on Early Rehabilitation in Patients with Ischemic Stroke TCM synthesis rehabilitation project. *Chinese Journal of Integrated Traditional and Western Medicine.*

2002,9(5): 288-289.

76. Zhang Jun, Huang Yan,Wang Yong-yan. The Key Point and the Advancement on the First-level and Secondary Prevention of Acute Ischemic Stroke in the Combination of TCM with Western Medicine. *Chinese Archives of Traditional Chinese Medicine.* 2002,9(3): 71-73.

77. Gao Yu, Geng Xiao-juan. To Explore the Change Rule of Wind-phlegm Syndrome of Ischemic Stroke. *Chinese Archives of Traditional Chinese Medicine.* 2000, 41(12): 723-725.

78. Fan Xue-cong, Dong Shao-long. Research Progress of Chinese Medicine in Treatment of Ischemic Stroke. *Journal of Liaoning University of Traditional Chinese Medicine.* 2005,4(22): 163-165.

79. Yang Yun-fang, BaiXue. Apoplexy Prevention and Treatment Advantages of Chinese Medicine. *Journal of Shandong University of Traditional Chinese Medicine.* 2004,11(2): 159.

80. Xiong Ying, Wu Yun-chuan, Jin Hong-zhu, Randomized controlled trials on the influence and mechanism of manipulation on delayed onset muscle soreness after eccentric exercise. *China Journal of Orthopaedics and Traumatology.* 2009,22(9): 1205-1206.

81. Lijian, Liu Wei-min, LiMing, LI-Quan. The effect analysis of early functional rehabilitation treatment on the hemiplegic patients suffering from stroke. *Foreign Medical Sciences: Physical Medicine and Rehabilitation*. 2004, 26(10): 610.

82. Zhou Yan-ping,Ouyang Qing-yi. Insomnia Treated with Chinese Medicine Therapy of Feet-bathing,Auricular-plaster: An Observation and Nursing of 80 Cases. *Chinese Journal of Integrated Traditional and Western Medicine*. 2008,7(26): 66-67.

83. Jiang Hai-hua. Exploration of "Treat Undisease" Theory is Applied to Prevention and Treatment in Stroke. *Chinese Archives of Traditional Chinese Medicine*. 2004,21(6): 470-473.

84. GuoJian-wen, Pan Feng, Li Jun-ya. Experimental Considerations on Ischemic Stroke Treated with Regulating Blood Sea of Brain through Ang/Tie2 Signal Pathway. *Chinese Journal of Basic Medicine in Traditional Chinese Medicine*. 2005,3(4): 319-320.

85. Li Wen-yang, Bao Yi-mei, LiYu-hua. Affect on Blood Rheology when using Acupuncture Method Therapy of Reinforcing Kidney, Regulating *Du Mai*, Strengthening Spleen, and Removing Stagnation in Ischemic Stroke. *Journal of Liaoning University of Traditional Chinese Medicine*. 2007,24(2): 101.

86. Liu Sheng-xue, GaoGe, Yuan Xia. The Application of Classified Diagnosis on Apoplexy Using Step-wise Discriminant Analysis. *Chinese Journal of Health Statistics*. 2006,23(5): 400-402.

87. Shao Feng-yang, Li Le-jun. Clinical Research Of Stroke Unit of Integrated Traditional and Western Medicine. *Chinese Archives of Traditional Chinese Medicine*. *Chinese Journal of Rehabilitation Medicine*. 2002,20(2): 153-154.

88. Wu Ping, Xiao Ding-hong. Clinical observation of "Bu Yang Huan Wu Tang-Decoction" in treating apoplectic sequelae of qi deficiency and blood stasis. *Shanghai Journal of Traditional Chinese Medicine*. 2009,21(1): 87-88.

89. Yang Qi-wang, Zhang Dong-shu. Acupuncture on Four Seas' Shu Points in the Treatment of Acute Ischemic Stroke. *Journal of Clinical Acupuncture and Moxibustion*. 2003, 7(10): 29-30.

Index

图书在版编目（CIP）数据

中风=Stroke：Help From Chinese Medicine：英文/迟慧彦等主编.—北京：人民卫生出版社，2012.4

（中医科普系列）

ISBN 978-7-117-11621-3

Ⅰ.①中… Ⅱ.①迟… Ⅲ.①中风-中医治疗法-英文 Ⅳ.①R255

中国版本图书馆CIP数据核字（2011）第202233号

门户网：www.pmph.com	出版物查询、网上书店
卫人网：www.ipmph.com	护士、医师、药师、中医师、卫生资格考试培训

中医科普系列—中风（英文）

主　　编：迟慧彦　卡尔·斯蒂姆森	
出版发行：人民卫生出版社（中继线＋8610-5978-7399）	
地　　址：中国北京市朝阳区潘家园南里19号	
邮　　编：100021	
网　　址：http://www.pmph.com	
E－mail：pmph@pmph.com	
发　　行：pmphsales@gmail.com	
购书热线：＋8610-5978-7338/7399（电话及传真）	
开　　本：850×1168　1/24	
版　　次：2012年4月第1版　2012年4月第1版第1次印刷	
标准书号：ISBN 978-7-117-11621-3/R·11622	

版权所有，侵权必究，打击盗版举报电话：＋8610-5978-7482

（凡属印装质量问题请与本社销售部联系退换）